WANDERERS ALL

BOOKS BY GREGORY ARMSTRONG

Wanderers All

"The Dragon Has Come"

WANDERERS ALL

An American Pilgrimage

GREGORY ARMSTRONG , 1931-

HARPER & ROW, PUBLISHERS

NEW YORK

HAGERSTOWN

SAN FRANCISCO

LONDON

*This book is for Virginia Hilu, my friend
and editor. The inspiration of her bravery
and grace will always be with me.*

FIRST EDITION

Designed by Sidney Feinberg

Library of Congress Cataloging in Publication Data

Armstrong, Gregory, 1931–
    Wanderers all.
    1. Armstrong, Gregory, 1931–   2.   United
States—Biography.   I.   Title.
CT275.A8218A38 1977   973.92′092′4   [B]   76–26210
ISBN 0–06–010139–3

77 78 79 80 10 9 8 7 6 5 4 3 2 1

All the boys and girls without fathers and mothers . . .
All the little wanderers who never give up searching . . .
All the strangers on earth who have lost their way . . .
How could they know that there is no way and that there
   never has been?
How could they know that no one ever finds the way?
How could they know that there never were any mothers
   or fathers?
Only other little wanderers like themselves.

G.A.

I am on my way. To what? A few scraps of paper? Perhaps. Does it matter? I dream of walking into the town where my father was born and seeing his face everywhere. In the faces of old men and women. In the faces of young girls. In the faces of infants in their carriages. According to the story I have been told about my father's past, there were eight other children in the family that gave my father up for adoption. If they all had children and their children had children, I would have hundreds of relatives in this one small town. My father's genes would be in all of them, grown into their cheekbones and noses just as they have grown into my own face. My newfound relatives would see themselves in me. I wouldn't have to explain myself. A few words and I would be accepted as one of them. And the darkness would begin to clear.

Maine

AFTER eating and finding a place to stay in Augusta, I walk down in the darkness to the Kennebec River.

According to the newspaper, there have been heavy rains and snows for over two weeks and the river is at its highest point since 1936. Supposedly there is danger of severe flooding. The swollen river can't catch up with itself. It dashes ahead, catches its breath and then batters against itself like chunks of solid matter hurled against an impenetrable wall. Ice is just starting to form on the surface of the water. In the moonlight, it looks like hundreds of skeins of silver hair.

The room where I am staying is unheated. By the time I get back, the temperature outside has dropped to twenty below. I lie in bed dressed in my clothes, covered with the three blankets and my overcoat, and still I shudder. My teeth chatter. And even though I'd much rather be warm, I say to myself that this is just the way it should be. It shouldn't be easy to unlock the past. I want to pay the whole price, whatever it turns out to be.

I am awed by my bravery at coming here. And the glow of expectancy on my face defies even the freezing cold.

Both my parents were orphans. They married the first night they met and stayed married to each other for the rest of their lives.

My father never made any attempt to find out who his real parents were. The worst had always happened to him. Presumably he felt there was no reason to tempt fate once more.

As a young child, my mother had known her parents. But for all the knowledge she was willing to reveal about them, it was almost as if they had never existed.

I have come here to Maine to find out all I can about their missing parents, the grandparents that I never knew. I don't know how far back the idea for this trip goes. In one way or another, it seems as if I have been preparing for it all my life. It is the culmination of a fantasy that has been brewing in me for as long as I can remember. A long-delayed puberty rite that I have to take care of before I can go on with the rest of my life.

My father was a secret orphan. My mother knew, but she conspired with him to keep it secret from both his children. It wasn't until I was eighteen that I discovered the actual circumstances of his birth. By accident, I found a letter and a card from the FBI among the playing cards and poker chips in a bureau drawer. During the war my father had been forced to get a security clearance. There on the card were the real names of his mother and father.

For a long time I pretended not to know. Perhaps I was even able to forget. If he needed to hide so badly, perhaps there was a reason, I said to myself, that I shouldn't know. Years later, in a conversation with my mother, the subject of orphans came up and I asked her about my father's birth. It turned out that he and his twin brother had been placed in an orphanage when they were two and a half years old. Sometime later they were adopted by a family that subsequently broke up and then a second time by an old Boston dowager whom I had always been led to believe was his real mother. I wasn't surprised not to have been told before. My father's whole life was a mystery to me.

My mother was almost blatantly an orphan. It was as if she felt that the pain of her life was so egregious that it had to have the benefit of some extraordinary explanation.

My mother's father was a sea captain who died when she was six. When I was growing up, she would talk about him in the language of a schoolgirl's daydreams. I was supposed to look just like him. I would have been named after him if my mother had had her way. Every so often she would show me a photo of him. A giant, bald-headed man standing on the parapet of the Morro Castle in Cuba, squinting in the sun like a stone gargoyle, solitary and unapproachable.

Of her own mother she never said a word. She never even mentioned her name. And yet it wasn't from lack of knowing her. Her mother lived for three years after her father died. But not one word about this woman, my maternal grandmother, did my mother ever tell me. Nor did she ever show me even a single photo or memento or trinket that had belonged to her mother. Not a single memory she could bring herself to share with her own children. She used to claim that her mother had died three years earlier than she actually had. Three years less of silence. Three years less of mystery.

It was after the death of her mother that my mother was forced to wander Cinderella-like from one poor relation to the next.

It was almost as if my parents felt their orphanness made them radioactive. No people could have been more hidden. They protected me from knowledge about themselves as if they believed they were carriers of a deadly virus which they would pass on to me.

I didn't know what it was that made us so different. All I knew was that we were a race apart. We lived as if at any minute a huge hand could appear and crush us for a minor infraction. Only us. No one else. It was our luck. Our fate. The Armstrong luck. Nothing had ever gone right for them. Nothing would ever go right for us. Nothing would ever go right for me.

Both of them lived as if they believed that other people were always better. People with parents. They took so little for themselves. The little they did take they took so apologetically. So deferentially. Despite his great talent, my father was never able to succeed in the world. It was almost as if he believed that orphans had no right to worldly success.

The worst of it was that they lived as if they had no right even to each other.

In spite of their best efforts, the sense of their orphans' stigma was passed on to me. I, too, became afraid to touch my own children just the same way my parents had been afraid to touch me. Somewhere deep inside myself, I believed that the most I could do for my children, the biggest gift that I could give to them, was to withhold myself from them. That was why I took such a small part in their lives. Why, in some sense, I made orphans out of them just the same way I had been orphaned by my own parents. To protect them from myself.

And now, here I am in Maine. I tell myself that I've come here to find my missing grandparents. But that is only a part of it.

Why not tell the truth for once? It's really very simple. I'm here because I don't know how to love. I'm here because I can't stand to go on being loveless anymore. Because, somehow, I feel that my lovelessness has something to do with never having had any roots. With the sense of orphanness that I have inherited.

I've cut myself off from my job. I've ended a career that has lasted almost twenty years. I've been separated from my wife for over six years. I haven't been able to stay with any woman since then for more than a few months at a time. I have no really close friends. I'm what is called a loner. A wanderer without any discernible roots. The silent one off in the corner. The one whose face is screwed up in painful perplexity because he has never quite understood what is going on around him.

After all these years, I'm still walking the streets of New York City alone at night. Walking to nowhere.

I'm not so naïve as to believe that I can discover what I have missed in life by going back into an unknown past. But I've tried everywhere else. This is what I am left with. This is where I will have to begin again.

=

In the diner across the street from my motel, where I go to have breakfast, everyone knows each other. All around me there is a patter of small talk like oatmeal sputtering. *Did you know that gas has gone up another five cents? Do you have enough heat? Have you seen Al since he got out of the hospital? He really looks great.* Everyone speaks and everyone listens, and yet no one really seems to care if they are heard.

When the waitress turns toward me, her face tightens. Her voice becomes hard and precise. She is not unfriendly. It is just that there is nothing shared between us. No common history. The others are old friends and I am the stranger.

After breakfast, I rent a small car and go bouncing along the icy streets. The Department of Health and Welfare, where the vital statistics are kept, turns out to be only a few blocks from my motel.

I explain to the clerk what I am trying to find.

"Oh, you are trying to trace your family tree." She smiles with friendly condescension.

"Yes, that's right." It is as good a way as any to describe what I am doing. But when I explain in more detail what I am trying to find, her face becomes troubled.

"Oh. If there is an adoption, I can't help you. All those records are sealed. There was a law passed in 1962."

My face falls. She notices my distress and moves to reassure me.

"Maybe there never was an adoption. That happens sometimes. You think there is one and it turns out there never was. Give me the name and I'll go back and look."

I write out the name my father had given me. *Cecil Burrows.* She walks to the back of an office and enters a door with a half-window. I see her walking back and forth. The longer she stays in that room, the more encouraged I become. When she finally emerges though, she is shaking her head.

"I can't find anything under that name. The birth records must have been placed in the adoption file. You will have to find a judge who will give you a court order to examine the records."

Suddenly it seems as if my trip has come to an end even before it has begun. Why would a judge give me a court order? I have no reason except sentiment. No reason except for the fact that I have been yearning for this information for over twenty-five years.

They are having a small Christmas party at the judge's office. The clerks are glowing with good cheer.

I explain myself and they are delighted with my story. I'm beginning to realize the magic of those words "family tree." One of the clerks goes off to find the judge. He turns out to be a twinkling little man in a business suit. I explain my errand. He thinks for a minute.

"I don't see what harm it could do. Even your father's adoptive parents must be dead by now. Just write down all the names you have and I'll give you an order to examine the records."

I write down the names I have for my father. Cecil Burrows, the name my father was given at birth. James Andrews, the name he was given when he was first adopted. Matthew Armstrong, the name by which I have always known him. The judge signs the paper with a Christmas flourish.

The clerk motions for me to wait. Fusses with some papers and then comes over to me smiling.

"I see you got it. Good for you."

I hand her the court order.

"I'll see what I can do for you. It will probably take a while. The records are kept in a number of different places."

Several times I notice her face in the window of the door as she walks back and forth. I try to imagine what is happening from her expression. When she finally returns, she has a piece of paper in her hand, but something is troubling her.

"I found something. It must be your father and his brother, but he never was adopted and his real name is not Burrows but Andrews. You didn't need a court order after all. There was nothing under those other names."

And she hands me a piece of paper with the names of my grandparents: Florence A. Kincaid, born Arbor, Maine. No date of birth. John A. Andrews, born East Northwood, New Hampshire. No date of birth. Two male children born on April 22, 1903. Cecil Arthur and Harold Albert Andrews. Physician, G. J. Nelson, China, Maine.

My father was never adopted. I wonder if he knows. I ask myself how he could have ever become confused about his original name. I can't believe that he would deliberately mislead me. And yet I wonder. He has kept that door closed for seventy-one years.

Now that I have had my first taste of success, I am greedy. But the clerk can't help me anymore. She doesn't have the time. The records are very difficult to work with. The only people who can go into the file room are six licensed genealogists. She gives me the name of the one closest by and I am on my way.

⊽

Before I came up here, I asked my father if he would give me his blessings for my journey. I thought he would say no. He has always said no to me all my life.

My father thought for a while. His chest heaved, his face turned ashen and he began to tremble. He gave me a look of sudden apprehension. I could see him wanting to say no, yet I knew he couldn't say it because he couldn't find any excuse to deny me. In a whisper, he told me that it was "all right." And then, in a voice choked with emotion, he went on.

"I should have probably gone myself. My brother Ronald talked about searching for our parents but I don't know what came of it. Perhaps he just didn't want to tell me if he did find something. Perhaps he thought it would be better if I didn't know."

I winced at this revelation of the depth of his dread. I asked him why he hadn't gone back himself. When he didn't reply, I suggested that it was probably because of his anger against his real parents for giving him up.

"No," he replied, "that wasn't true. The real reason was that I was afraid they might be hard up and I didn't want them sponging off me."

I thought, so that is what he has been telling himself all these years, knowing that he couldn't really believe those words.

Later on, I persuaded my mother to let me borrow some pictures from the family album. I found an aging sepia photo of my father and his brother wearing embroidered dresses, standing on the lawn of an awesome mansion. They looked so out of place. The figures seemed almost as if they had been cut out of another photo and pasted onto a new background. It must have been taken only a few months after they left the orphanage. There was another photo of my father and his brother many years later when I was nine months old. I was perched on my father's knee. His brother held my hand. The men were beautiful and sleek as seals glistening with water in the sunlight. I also found a photo of my mother when she was twenty, tall and slender, her clothes falling about her like a waterfall, holding my little hands in hers as I stood between her legs, a fat blond imp. She looks up at the camera almost as if she were begging forgiveness for so much joy.

I also wanted them to find the document which contained my father's original name. As my father searched for it, I got the strangest feeling that he knew where it was and that he was just pretending to search for it. We had to go through a charade of thumbing through a huge bundle of miscellaneous papers, mortgages, canceled insurance policies, old leases. Yet I was certain that he knew just as well as I did that it was hidden under the glossy paper that lines his dresser drawer. I couldn't admit that I knew where it was because I didn't want to reveal how well I knew the hidden contents of their house. Nor did I want to bring his mixed feelings out into the open again.

As I watched him going back and forth pretending to search, the veil of fatherhood was lifted from him for just a moment. He seemed like a small mouse scurrying desperately for a niche or a crack in the wall in which he could hide. And I knew deep down that he didn't want me to go to Maine. I knew that he really just wanted me to go away and leave him alone. But he couldn't bring himself to say those words. Nor could I bring myself to say them for him.

I knew my mother was also very apprehensive about what I might discover about her own parents. As I closed the front door behind me, I looked around and saw her walking away from the door. Just a moment before, when she knew I was looking at her, her face had been glowing. But when she thought I had turned away, that look of pleasure was suddenly replaced by a look of bleak despair.

I thought I knew her so well. And yet I really don't know her at all. Because that face that I saw was utterly strange to me. I suspect it is the inner face of her self. The face of her self that she is the only one to see.

⬇

The street where Naomi Grant, the genealogist, lives is on the outskirts of Augusta. A street of utter stillness where people grow old in silence. Where no children play and there are no raucous noises. A street of canes and faltering footsteps. Small frame houses that probably go back a hundred years. Aged, yellowing lace curtains. People themselves like wisps of lace peering through the windows.

When she opens the door, I know she is really seeing me. No reticence about looking me straight in the eye. I am a strange person and she intends to get the full benefit of my unexpected appearance. Yellowish white hair. Puckered wrinkled skin that must be soft as satin. When I tell her why I have come, she invites me in. I walk very softly because the house seems almost as frail as her emaciated body.

"You know, I'm eighty-nine and it's hard for me to get around. I've got a very bad knee and I have to use this cane."

I look down but her knee is covered by the folds of her faded floral print dress. I find myself whispering to her, turning down the volume of my life so its New York intensity won't break or shatter the cobwebs of her house. I try to make myself old and slow so I won't disturb anything in that house, so that I can survive in that ancient air which hangs so heavily around me.

I follow her upstairs to the room where she has her office. She pulls out book after book of names that she has compiled over the years from old records of births, deaths and marriages. Names she has copied from tombstones in graveyards from all over the state. Names have been her whole life. She has never married or had any children. But in that room she has thousands of ancestors to keep her company. She doesn't seem to think about anything more than the names. Not how their possessors lived or who they were. Just their names. Yet somehow those old names must speak to her of faraway places and of fabulous dreams.

We settle down in our chairs in her study and she begins reading off name after name, telling me where she found each one. I begin to realize what it is she really does. She gives people their pasts. They come to her just as I have and she gives them wondrous dreams. To people who are cut off from themselves and the present of their lives, to nameless people like myself, she is the obstetrician of our history. She gives people whole families, flocks of relations. She makes us all the inheritors, the repositories of the past. We listen to her and suddenly we matter because all these other people have given their lives for us. They all lived so that we could live. All their lives are somehow inside us. As she reads my names, I get a sense of being part of an extended human history. And the names she reads are not even necessarily connected to me in any way, not even necessarily the names of my relatives. Just an assemblage of Andrews and Kincaids who lived and died and gave birth before the beginning of the twentieth century. Abigail and Isaiah Andrews, who married on July 22, 1857. Florilla, who married on July 16, 1876. Among all the Franks and Georges are wonderful odd flowers like Samantha. Could she have been a witch? My daughter, Mary, always wanted a new name. Perhaps that could be it. And Captain John, who died in Arbor, Maine, on October 30, 1846, and who had two daughters, Mary and Harriet. Was he a real captain or an impostor? Somehow I see him with a peg leg. Was he a pirate or a buccaneer? Names, names, names. But none of them conclusively mine. So far as we can tell, none of them related to Florence Kincaid or to John A. Andrews.

Each time she brings out a new book, I become excited all over again. But finally there are no more books and none of those hundreds of names they contain lead to anything. Each name now seems to deprive me of my past because it doesn't belong to me. When the last book is closed, we are silent for a while. She tells me I shouldn't be discouraged. She really didn't expect to find anything. It was just a chance she wanted to take because I was there. Sometimes you can get lucky. If I want her to, she can go back to the Hall of Records and she will be almost certain to find something. But I'll have to wait a week.

She suggests that I go to Arbor if I have time and check through the records myself. I tell her that I will because I am thinking about writing a book about my search for the past. A twinkle comes into her eyes.

"I've always thought someone should write a book about me."
And she begins to tell me the story of her life.

Once, with another girl, she discovered a hornet's nest in a dead tree. She told her friend not to move, but her friend ran and the bees bit her on the legs. But Naomi didn't move and she wasn't bitten.

When she was growing up, there were ice-skating parties on the lake. After hours of skating the lads and their young ladies would collapse on the benches around roaring log fires, sitting there like wilted flowers.

I ask her if the boys were shy.

"No. Country boys are never shy."

There were also hay rides in the summer. The orphanage was not far away. In the spring, nine months after the hay rides, the girls' babies would be born and taken to the orphanage. I wonder to myself if this wasn't the way my father and his brother were conceived.

Her father was a country minister. Once someone came to town and told him about a man and a woman who had been living together for about fifteen years and had a "mess of children." Her father said, "I'll see what I can do." He went out and talked to them and one day they came to church.

"The man was dressed in overalls and the woman wore a Mother Hubbard. All their children were with them. After my father performed the ceremony, the man gave him a fifty-cent piece. My father turned it back, saying, 'I suspect you need this more than I do.'

"Someday," Miss Grant went on, "I want to write a book, *Recollections of a Parson's Daughter.*" And I think to myself what a wonderful book that will be.

We go downstairs. Before I leave, I ask if I can give her a kiss. And she offers me her cheek. I am right. It is as soft as satin.

⏐

When I was young, I was always searching for the answers to secrets. Particularly I was searching for the answers I thought my parents were keeping from me. Why was I bad? Why did my father hate me? What was so special about me that my mother had to treat with such dread?

I usually went searching in the afternoon when I was supposed to be sleeping. "Taking a nap" was what my mother called it. It was supposed to be good for me. Everything I did was supposed to be good for me.

My grainy fingers would sink deep into the recesses of their bureau drawers. I would poke them into my mother's underwear, soft antique satin, rose-colored satin. My fingers would slip through them as if I were touching air. I always believed that she would know that I had been into her drawer because my feeling of touching all those forbidden things was so strong. I suspected that traces of my presence would remain, and that the places where I touched them would shine in the dark with the marks of my hands.

So many mysteries. The cotton pads with the cloth strips at either end like Band-Aids. I used to tear them apart, one after the other, hoping to discover whatever was hidden inside. A kernel of something or other. A jewel.

Smell of talcum sent flying as I ruffled through layers of muslin. So soft to my fingers. As if my fingers could be lost forever in its softness. Feeling sightlessly in the darkness of the drawers, rings, old coins, stickpins, litter of pennies. Mystical coins because they had lain in that place for so long with locks of hair that frightened me because hair, other people's hair, seemed to hold the contagion of death. Uncovering little folded papers with gold scrollwork in glassine envelopes. To this day I still don't know what they were. And that sticky antique dust that falls from our lives and collects in drawers and which seems to have a fungoid life of its own, which I could rub into little balls between my damp fingers. That lint and the knots of hair were the most forbidden secrets of all because they seemed to contain the very essence of my mother and father. It seemed so unbearably intimate to be able to fondle those coagulated, dampish essences of their beings—the very effluvia from their groin hairs, where I always found it on myself.

In time I found other things in the dark recesses of closets,

14

hidden in boxes underneath Christmas tree ornaments and rotting piles of lace. A .22-caliber pearl-handled revolver. I used to press its cold barrel against my forehead in the summer. The bullets used to tinkle and clatter like marbles in the palm of my hand.

Then there was my mother's diaphragm in its special box. When I opened it, a cloud of talcum powder rose up to my nostrils. I used to love to rub my fingers over it. Especially the knuckles of my fingers where the feeling of strangeness was so intense. I couldn't figure out what to do with it. I knew it wasn't a balloon. But somehow I thought it should be. I never could figure out how to inflate it. The way it was tucked away and cherished so carefully in its special blue box meant that it had to be something very powerful and strange. Sometimes I would stretch it over my face like a rubber mask, like a second skin. Covering my pores so my skin couldn't breathe, sucking in the aromas of rubber and talcum. On one of those exploring days, I poked a small hole in it. Just a microscopic hole with one of those round-headed pins that I found in another part of the drawer. Was I the one who gave birth to my brother? With one incisive stroke of that strange pin that I also used to slip under the first layer of skin on one of my fingers, where it would rest like a small blue vein? Sometimes I would take other pins and stick them in my other fingers, entranced by the black lines they would make under my skin. Dark worms burrowing inside me.

⇌

And now so many years later I am still searching for the same answers. It isn't only my missing grandparents I am trying to find. Not so long ago, I started to persuade my parents to talk to me about their own lives.

When I first started visiting them, I didn't think that my father would ever talk to me about himself or that my mother would ever talk about herself in front of him, so I chose times when I knew my mother would be alone or my father would be napping. I thought that if I was lucky, I could also persuade her to talk to me about my father.

Very quickly my mother and I got back into our childhood

game, into our old roles as secret lovers. The first time I arrived, my father was still awake. At the first hint of drowsiness, a drooping eyelid or falling chin, my mother reminded my father that it was time for him to go upstairs. And when he didn't leave quickly enough, she made dire predictions about what would happen to him.

"You know how you get if you don't take your nap. You'll be tired for days afterward and perhaps you won't even be able to breathe."

Her voice quivered with concern. But we all knew that what she was really saying was "Go away so I can be alone with my son."

When, finally, grudgingly, he left the room, my mother began. She went on for hours without stopping. I listened with one ear cocked for the sound of my father stirring upstairs, hoping that he wouldn't awaken until she had exhausted her recollections.

"We got married the first night we met. I was sixteen and your father was twenty-four. I had been expecting another man. He couldn't come and your father came in his place. I had only seen him once before when my Cousin Valerie pointed him out to me."

When she met him, she was wearing the classic young girl's costume of the day ("I'd have died if anyone thought I looked different")—a short skirt, long beads, unbuttoned arctics and a yellow slicker with graffiti written all over it which she had bought with the money she earned after school working in an electroplating company. He was driving a Stutz Bearcat, wearing a derby hat and a raccoon coat. Costumes are so important to people. When everything else is forgotten, memories of the costumes still remain.

"I was living with Uncle Rob and Aunt Sue. I was scared to death of Rob. Just the week before, he had beaten me up one night and the next morning I had found pieces of my scalp on the kitchen floor.

"My cousin Valerie used to beat me too. Once she took my clothes and threw them away. She was constantly hitting me and using bad language. Insulting me in front of my friends.

"Because she had no friends of her own, she forced me to go out on double dates with her. She broke up all my friendships. She was

16

always humiliating me. Once, when I was wearing a coat that my Cousin Martha had sent me, Valerie shoved me in the snow and muck in front of everyone. Another time she beat me with a belt buckle and blood spurted from my shoulder."

I have heard some of this before but, as always when my mother talks about the painfulness of her childhood, my head swims. Everything seems to liquefy in front of my eyes. My beautiful mother abused. Brutalized. This image of my mother is one of her deepest legacies to me.

"It was on Thanksgiving night we got married. Before Rob left to spend some time at the bar where he used to drink, he told me and my Cousin Valerie that we couldn't go out, even though he knew we had dates with men who were coming all the way from Boston. Valerie insisted we go anyway. She said we would be sure to be back before he returned. I was almost as afraid of Valerie as I was of Rob. Never having any way of my own. No right to preferences. I always had to fit into the desires of others.

"Rob's wife, Sue, said we could go if we were sure to be back before ten. So, reluctantly, I agreed to go. The idea was that we would go to a place to get some sandwiches and coffee and then come right home. But all the places were crowded and by the time we got served, it was already past ten.

"I told Valerie, 'Your father must be home by now. You know what will happen to your mother if we are not there. I'm terrified.'

"Your father said, 'But he can't do anything to you.'

"I replied, 'But you don't know this man.' And I described what had happened the week before.

"I said to Valerie, 'What are we going to do? I'm afraid to go home.' I wasn't even thinking about the men. Someone said, let's get married. We all talked for a while and the men got very serious. Your father had a hundred-dollar bill. He always carried a hundred-dollar bill in his wallet. Valerie and I were both terrified. But we didn't know what else to do."

My mother is such a great storyteller. Her eyes sparkle. She loves the melodrama. The pungent details. The high romance of it all.

"First we all went to a hotel in New Haven and got separate

rooms. I began to get cold feet. I said to Valerie, 'Hadn't we better get out of it?'

"Valerie said we had no choice and told me to shut up.

"The men tried to be sweet. They bought us soap and toothbrushes. The next day we all went down to Athens, New York. At seven that night, we found a minister in a hardware store.

"Pop was very sweet. I knew he wasn't going to be mean. I'd started it. He had a job. I wasn't going to make a fool of him by leaving him. He waited three weeks before he laid a hand on me. But all I wanted to do was fly away.

"His foster mother knew even before he called to tell her. Rob had called and told her everything, including my age.

"Your father turned from the phone and looked over at me queerly.

" 'How old are you?' he asked.

"I had told him eighteen. But this time I told him the truth. I was really sixteen.

" 'Do you know that you could have gotten me in trouble? They could get me on the Mann Act. You're not allowed to take an underage girl out of the state.'

"His foster mother told him to take me home immediately because I was just a child.

"The Boston *American* ran a story with a picture:

GIRLS QUIT SCHOOL TO STAGE A DOUBLE ELOPEMENT.

"His foster mother tore up the picture. She was very angry. But after a week or so, she relented and asked us to tea. Her first words to him were 'Matthew, I don't know whether to congratulate you or take a stick to you.'

"Tea was served by one of the maids. Cold cuts. Two kinds of salad, vegetable and Waldorf. Cream cheese and Bar-le-Duc (that's French currant jelly). Hot biscuits. Several different kinds of cake and homemade ice cream.

"As we were leaving, his foster mother called me over and reminded me that it was customary for the bride's parents to provide the silver and the linen. Since I didn't even have anybody to give me so much as a pin cushion, I just wanted to get away from there as fast as I could."

At that moment, we heard my father coming downstairs. My mother fell silent. When he entered the room, we both looked away from him and fell into ourselves. He sat in a chair and, still groggy from sleep, waited for us to return.

⇌

It is already beginning to get dark by the time I leave Augusta. I have been told that there is no place to spend the night in Arbor, so I am driving to Lakeland. Coming over the bridge that divides the two towns, I see a huge smokestack towering over the trees, with an enormous plume of pearl-gray smoke frozen and motionless above it like an elongated oyster, curved and plump and ever so faintly swelling against the black-blue sky.

Further on, I pass an ancient motel called The Yankee Clipper that resembles an old hunting lodge. I go inside and register.

Later I decide to go into town to eat. I find a modern, overlit coffee shop in a shopping center. I am the last customer. An old lady serves me very reluctantly. Perhaps she could be my grandmother. I think how badly she will feel about not being more friendly if it turns out that I am her grandson.

When I finish, I go out into the street. The town is closed. The streets are empty. The only sound is of a damp reverberation. There are faint umbrellas of light from the street lamps on the dark macadam pavement.

I decide to go down to the river. Past a blaze of light from a small hotel. I slip down the loose dirt on the upper banks and down the steep side in the total darkness to the very edge of the water. White foaming floodwater surges down a precipice and under a bridge. Roars in my ears. Warm yellow rectangles of light glow in the windows of a factory building off in the distance. Masses of black debris lurch past me and tumble over the precipice and then continue on their way. The dam has burst and everything around me and inside me is loose and flowing.

I stand there for what seems like hours, agog with fear and

expectancy, and then drive back to my room with the sense of wonder and promise vibrating all around me.

In the morning, a fine dust of snow swirls in waves and funnels across the pavement outside my window. As I drive over to Arbor, the snow curls and prances around my car.

The city hall is a brick and glass building like the wing of a modern hospital. A place where the poetry of expectations ends. Fluorescent tubes. No shadows, no darkness, no ghosts. Inside, a plastic Santa Claus is propped up against a wall. Bits of tinsel have been strung from the ceiling.

The county clerk's office is just one large room. Off in one corner, three plump women talk and drink coffee. A cheap phono plays Christmas music. Country music comes from another corner of the room from a small radio. All the sounds blend together like the sputtering of a huge caldron of soup.

The county clerk's desk is empty, so I walk over to the women and stand beside them. But even though they have seen me, they go on talking as if they didn't even know I was there. They bark words at each other like terriers. No one listens. Nothing relates to anything else. Each one makes sure she gets her chance to bark just as much as any of the others.

I am just a little boy who has wandered into a coffee klatsch in someone's kitchen, because all men are boys to women like these. No matter what a man says, they only smile patronizingly. Because men don't have enough sense to stay in the kitchen and drink coffee and talk. Because men think they can accomplish something important in the world. And these women know the folly of that.

Finally, I break in and ask for the clerk. The three of them turn their heads toward me simultaneously, each with the same look of amazement on her face. As if to say: *How could you dare to break in on us that way?*

"She's just gone out. She'll be back in a while."

As if to deliberately contradict my paranoia, they smile very invitingly and offer me a cup of coffee. I shake my head. I don't want to become one of those ladies drinking coffee in the morning.

"Well, just sit down and wait. She'll be back in a while."

I pace back and forth. There is no chair for me. But those women will always have a place. Everywhere they go, a coffee table miraculously appears, complete with sweet rolls and toast. And if I find her, I suppose that my grandmother will be one of those women too. It is inevitable.

After a long while the clerk finally arrives. She is almost preternaturally young. Someone who has grown into middle age and married and had children and who is still just as schoolgirlish as she was thirty years ago. Behind a crust of fat and anxiety, she still has the melting ingenuous smile of a teenager. I show her the birth certificate I have brought with me from Augusta and explain what I am trying to do.

What are you telling me this for? her expression seems to say, I go on to explain in more detail how I am trying to discover my ancestry. I see a look of relief forming in her eyes. She opens her mouth and forms an "O" with her lips. Then she blows the sound at me.

"Oh, you are trying to trace your family tree."

Smiling the way a teacher smiles at a difficult pupil who has finally gotten the right answer. As if to say: *Why didn't you just tell me right off?* Now, in spite of the fact that I talk too fast and have long hair, I have an acceptable identity.

"Sit down just for a second and then we can get to work. I'm going to have to leave in a couple of hours, but we should be able to get a lot done before then." She takes up some papers and leaves the room. In a few seconds, she returns smiling with anticipation.

"Sit down here and I'll get out some of the records." She pulls over a chair so we can both sit together at her desk. For the first time I notice a bookcase filled with piles of old ledgers titled "Births," "Marriages" and "Deaths." The only items which are of note in so many lives. Sometimes not even a marriage, just a birth and a death.

"I hope we'll find something here. All the records before 1896 are down in the state archives in Augusta." She brings the ledgers over to the desk and we begin. "Marriages. 1896–1905, Arbor, Maine."

The first few pages have the names entered in alphabetical order with numbers referring to the page where the complete entry occurs. I run my eyes down the columns of names transcribed in the fine, spidery handwriting of the time. The clerk watches me, and the speed of my eyes bothers her.

"You've got to read very slowly because sometimes the names are misspelled." With a faint air of irritation, she takes the book from me.

Almost immediately, she finds a name. The pages flutter under her fingers. But it's just a false start. A wrong Andrews. The moving tip of her finger eats up the names in huge gulps, like a sponge taking up water. Another name. This time a Kincaid. Another false start. Now there are just two columns of names left.

Oh, I can tell by the look on her face that she has found something. Florence Kincaid and J. A. Andrews, laborer, were married on April 23, 1899, in China, Maine. She was seventeen and he was twenty-one. A chill runs up my back. The clerk smiles over at me benevolently. She doesn't say the words but her look says it all: *I'm so happy for you.* My great-grandparents' names are also listed. John B. Andrews of Northwood, New Hampshire, and Nellie Ross of Gardiner, Maine. I copy it all down as if it might get away from me if I don't transcribe it instantly.

Sensing my euphoria, the clerk tries to bring me back to earth.

"Now we want to find out if they had any other children, so we'll look at the birth records. I'll do that. You keep on going through the marriages, because you can never tell what you'll find. Maybe one of them died and the other got remarried. You can't leave any stone unturned."

I go on with the marriages. 1900. 1901. 1902. 1903. 1904. Hoping that I am not missing anything, but not really knowing what else I could possibly find. 1905. 1906. Then there it is. Florence Andrews was married to John Hamlin on June 13, 1906. I look and look again. There is no mistake. So my grandfather died and that is why my grandmother gave up her children. My grandfather is dead and I never knew him and I never will know him. I show my discovery to the clerk.

"If he was still alive, he would be ninety-six." But I think to myself how young he must have been when he died. It must have been in 1905. That meant he was only twenty-seven. My grandmother was only twenty-three and already a widow. She wouldn't have married until at least a year after his death.

But something is beginning to trouble me. I remember being told that the reason my father's real parents had given him up was because they had eight children and couldn't afford to keep the twins because they were too poor. But this is so different. If they were married in 1899, they couldn't possibly have had eight children by 1905, when my father was supposed to have been given up for adoption. Why wouldn't his foster mother have told him if it was because his father died? I shake my head. Then I see the clerk's face light up.

"You have an uncle." And she points to the place in the ledger where the entry of a birth has been made. She is like a nurse announcing to a father that he has a new son.

"His name is Hernando. Hernando Albourne Andrews." I ask myself how my grandmother could ever have found a name like that for a child born in Maine on November 2, 1899. Could she have ever been in love with a gypsy? I count the months from the marriage to the birth of the child. Less than seven, so of course they had to get married. I think back to what Naomi Grant told me: *Country boys are never shy,* and everything seems to make beautiful sense. I copy down the new name on my yellow pad and ask the clerk how my grandmother could have ever found such a strange name.

"Were there any Spanish people living around here then?"

"You never can tell where they get their names from." And I detect a note of professional irritation in her voice, as if she regarded the parents of children as so many blue jays picking up strange bits of thread and bringing in all those weird names no one had ever heard of before and expecting her to get them straight and to know how to spell them. They. They. They. Those others. The ones on the other side of the counter who come in and bother you and then go out and copulate like rabbits with no consideration for the people whose job it is to transcribe their outlandish names in the proper places.

But the twinge of irritation passes almost instantly and we both take a deep breath and go back to the ancient pages. We have solved the mystery. Now all the pieces will fall into place. One minute everything had seemed so random and fortuitous. Now the miracle of life's coherence and relatedness has been revealed.

In a few more minutes, she looks up again. "I think I've found something else. You have an aunt named Reena." And she points to the place on the page where the entry has been made and passes me the book so that I can copy down all the information. She watches me carefully, making sure I get it all straight, because something about me still doesn't strike her as being completely reliable.

Reena B. Andrews, born August 1, 1901. Parents, Florence Kincaid and J. A. Andrews, laborer. She could still be alive. She would be only seventy-three. She could actually be one of those three ladies sitting on the other side of the room.

"I've found your father." She points to the place in the book where those strange names have been written. Not Matthew and Ronald, but Cecil and Harold Andrews. For just an instant I have a sense of trespassing where I don't belong. It is almost the way I felt one day when I watched my father sleeping. As if I had no right to see him when he wasn't conscious and able to protect himself. My mind wanders back to the times when my father used to fall asleep on the floor in the living room on Sundays and we would all have to step over him as if he were a log.

The clerk's voice brings me back to the present.

"I have to do something now. I'll just leave you here with the books. I'll be back in half an hour." She smiles at me, apologetic for leaving me alone. After she goes, I just sit there musing for a while. The past is mine. I'm not a bit impatient for more. Somehow I know it will all come to me now.

But after a few minutes of dreaming, I take up the book of marriages and go on. Suddenly I find what I least expected. There is my grandfather's name again. John A. Andrews. On April 4,

1911, he married Mamie Lynn, daughter of Albert Lynn. Now he describes himself as a carpenter.

So he didn't die. He and Florence must have been divorced. Now the mystery of why my father and his brother were given up returns. It seems odd to me that people in rural areas could get divorces back at the turn of the century. I get the first faint suggestion that my relatives were real people and not the stereotypes I had brought with me to Maine.

So my grandmother and my grandfather were divorced. This seems like such an awesome fact. It means they were unhappily married. I know about that. I have been married too. So perhaps they were people just like me. At least they suffered and that is more than I ever expected to know about them.

Sitting there, I start to daydream. Mamie Lynn. I see her with a straw hat and tight blond curls. A coquette who flaunts her beauty. Tantalizing men. Swinging hips. I wonder what it must have been like for my grandfather to be walking with his new wife and to meet Florence, who sounds so prim and proper. Maybe he even married Mamie just to rub salt in Florence's wounds.

When the clerk returns, I tell her what I have found. She explains that divorces at that time weren't as uncommon as I might think. But I suspect her of just trying to humor me.

"From here on it will be very fast because it is all on cards in alphabetical order. I typed them out myself." Smiling as if she had done it just for me. Quickly she thumbs through the cards. No more births. Not for the Andrews or the Hamlins or the Lynn/Andrews. No more marriages. Only the discovery of a great-uncle, Ike Kincaid, my grandmother's brother, who married an Elizabeth Maxwell on May 2, 1920.

But the deaths start coming. Florence died in February, 1948. No listing of John A. Andrews's death, though. My Uncle Hernando died on May 13, 1953. The clerk holds the small white card in her hand and looks over at me with an inexplicable compassion.

"There is something that I shouldn't tell you." She waits for a sign. I catch her eyes.

"Oh, you can tell me." As if to say that I can take anything.

She sighs. "Your uncle committed suicide." She looks away, not wanting to be the one to have told me. As if it would really matter to me that someone I have never even met committed suicide.

I smile at her reassuringly. "Perhaps he was sick."

There is nothing more for us to do. No more names to look at. Timidly I offer her money for her time. But she doesn't want to take it from me. We have shared so much. She explains the difference. The only time she takes money is when people just write in and make her do all the work herself. Sometimes she resents it and wants to be paid. But it's different when people actually take the trouble to come in.

As I leave, the ladies at the other end of the room wave at me. Outside the snow is getting very deep.

Back in my motel room, I look up the names of all the Kincaids and Andrews and Lynns in the Arbor phone book and in all the surrounding areas. I decide to call them all.

Then I see one particular name that rings a bell. Elizabeth Kincaid. Who else could it be but my great-uncle's widow? I look for the location on my map and discover that it is not very far away. I look out the window and the snow seems to have abated.

Should I call or should I just go? I decide to go ring her doorbell and astonish us both.

The snow is about four inches deep now, but the car still holds the road. I find the street, but I can't seem to find the house number. At a certain point all the houses just seem to disappear. I can't understand what I am doing wrong. Why is it so difficult for me to find the house? Do I have such deep reservations about uncovering my past?

I decide to go back to a country store I passed and see if I can get some help.

"Why, the paper company bought that land and destroyed all the houses. Who are you looking for?"

I give him the name. He turns to someone else in the store and asks, "Doesn't so-and-so go with her daughter? Isn't she the one whose husband died just a few years ago?"

"Oh, yes. She lives down on Maple now."

He turns to me. "Have you got a phone number?" He dials, but the phone has been disconnected. He calls the phone company and gets another number. But still he gets no answer.

"Try her after supper. She's probably at work now." Obviously he is used to running the whole town from the control board of his store.

The snow is coming down very heavily now. My car is like an igloo. All the windows are covered with a layer of fine white crystals. It is as if I am the only person in the world. As the wipers cross the windshield, my isolation ends for just a second. But before they can sweep back again, I am in total seclusion from the world. Though I am frightened at not being able to see, my fear appears and disappears in waves which come and go to the rhythm of the windshield wiper. I am actually very happy inside my white-mantled womb. Outside, everything is covered with a deep layer of snow. The sky itself is thick with snow. And there seems to be no separation between myself and the rest of the world.

I am at one with everything. It's very peaceful to go on driving along the road, trusting almost entirely to instinct to get me to where I want to go. Feeling somehow that in spite of everything I must know my way, because I have been here before in the lives of my ancestors. That so many of my kind have tramped this very land where I am driving now.

And I am so warm and smug and euphoric. I can't see, but I know my way. As I turn the corners, the car almost seems to be turning itself. It seems to know where it is going.

⍦

The next time I visited my mother, she told me about her cousin and namesake, Cousin Martha, who acted as her fairy godmother.

"After Mama died, she kept a close watch on me."

My mother worshiped her. She was everything my mother ever hoped to be. A great beauty. A show girl. A singer on Broadway. She had even been married to a Swedish count.

Three months after my mother's marriage, Cousin Martha had come to Boston to meet my father. They were staying in a small cottage just outside the city. At one point during her visit, Cousin Martha asked my father to step outside so she could talk to my mother alone. For the next three hours, Cousin Martha tried to persuade her to leave my father. He stood outside crying. Cousin Martha even offered to pay for the divorce. But all my mother could think of was that man outside the window crying. She didn't want to embarrass him in front of his friends.

I didn't ask my mother what Cousin Martha thought was wrong with my father. I suppose I thought I knew. But as she went on, I began to guess what the real reasons were.

Like her cousin, my mother was also a great beauty. Long curly hair. A winsome, melting smile. Eyes that begged for love.

Cousin Martha had been promising to take her to New York when she was old enough and get her on the stage. Make her the darling of Broadway. Trips to Europe. Playboys. Nightclubs. They weren't just idle words. Cousin Martha's name was mentioned in all the gossip columns. Once she even made the front page of the *Daily News* after she jilted a wealthy Wall Street broker and he killed himself in the bathtub.

When my mother told me her dream about getting on Broadway, she suddenly became real to me in a way she had never been before. It was almost like seeing a figure in a painting shaking itself into life. For an instant, she wasn't my mother. She was a girl separate and distinct to me. A totally strange human being whom I would never be able to understand.

For an instant she was beautiful, her eyelashes glittering with tears, just the way she must have been then. So poised for life. So hopelessly expectant.

⩤

After supper, I start calling Elizabeth's number. Of course I have to call her Elizabeth. Already I have staked a claim to my relatedness with her.

The third time, a young girl answers the phone. She is very curious. Why am I calling her mother? Am I trying to make trouble for her? I realize that in a small town, everyone almost always knows who is going to call. There must be something faintly disturbing about an unfamiliar voice, because it suggests the possibility of disaster.

I mention that I am a distant relative. But that doesn't seem to satisfy her. So I tell her about my father and his brother, hoping that she won't think I am an eccentric and hang up the phone because my whole story seems so improbable. But she knows.

"Oh, my mother has told me about that." There is wonder and surprise in her voice. I can tell that she is beginning to sense that she is in the presence of something unusual and interesting. "Oh, my mother will really want to talk to you." Her voice becoming radiant. When I ask her about herself, she falters.

"Oh, I'm just in my last year of high school. My other two sisters have married." But I can tell that she doesn't want to talk about herself with a strange man.

"Look, my mother will be back in just a little while. I know she'll want to talk to you." Reluctantly, I agree to call back later.

When I call back, a woman's voice answers.

"Hello."

"Is this Elizabeth Kincaid?"

"Yes, this is Elizabeth Kincaid." She replies in a widow's voice which seems to have gaping holes in it, just like a scarecrow's coat. I explain who I am and why I am calling.

"Yes, Karla told me about it." Her daughter is very precious to her. The name is set off with a special reverence.

"Elizabeth." I insist on the intimacy of our relationship. "I'd like to see you."

"Oh, I'm not the person you should talk to." Speaking very slowly and choosing her words carefully, as if she were aware of a special responsibility in being the spokesman for the family, she explains that her husband was actually the son of Ike Kincaid. She just happened to have the same name as her mother-in-law. "I really don't know anything. I never knew the twins. My husband used to talk about them, but I don't think he'd ever met them either. The person you want to talk to is Ina. She would be your grandmother's sister. I have just called her and she wants to talk to you." She gives me Ina's phone number.

"Were there any other sisters?"

"Yes." Very precise. "There is Millie, Mildred. And Bessie."

"Could you give me their addresses?"

"Yes. But the one you should talk to is Ina." I write down the other addresses, wondering to myself why it is so important that I talk only to Ina and if they are trying to hide something from me.

I am reluctant to end the conversation for fear something important will elude me.

"I hope I can see you too."

"I'm sure you will." But there is no real desire in her voice. "Ina is the one you should talk to. She is waiting for you to call."

I put down the phone and lie back on the bed. So my past is really here. Not just names and dates in old ledgers, but the living memories of live human beings. My grandmother's three sisters are still alive.

In the face of so much reality I am actually trembling. I have to call. But I am apprehensive. There is no way to turn back now.

"Hello. Is this Ina Weston?"

"Yes."

"My name is Gregory Armstrong and I think I am related to you. I think you are my grandmother's sister." And I go on to tell her the story of my father and his twin brother.

"Yes. I know. Elizabeth told me about you and that you might be going to call." Her voice has the quality of ancient ivory. "I've always wondered what happened to the twins. Hardly a day passes but I don't think about them. I was only ten at the time, but I remember them so well."

"When can I see you?"

"You could come over now, but it's a little late. We're just getting ready for bed. It would be better if you could come over in the morning."

"I'll be there."

Long silence.

"This isn't any kind of trick, is it? I've always prayed that this moment would come."

I reassure her that I am real and we say good night.

⊽

The next time I visited my mother, we talked about her own childhood.

"After Mama died, I had to go live with Aunt Belle and Uncle John. Belle had arthritis and sat all day in the rocker, weeping. After a while, John, poor man, started acting strangely. He'd just up and start crying like Belle. Finally he had to take a leave of absence from his job and go into a sanitarium.

"When I was living with them, every day after school I would go down to the crossroads to watch the dining cars go by with their white tablecloths, hoping to be able to go away on one of them someday. Saying to myself, 'Will I ever?'

"I would read the society columns and cut out items and make up stories with paper dolls, using the names I found in a discarded Social Register. I also liked cutting out photos of people embarking for Europe.

"Most kids would have bedtime stories read to them. I would read children's stories to myself from the newspaper.

"One day John called up from the local train station to say that he had been released from the hospital and that he was on his way home. Aunt Belle was so happy. I was happy too. I really liked John. About half an hour later, the phone rang again. Shortly after answering it, my aunt fell off her chair.

"The call was from the depot. John had drunk carbolic acid in the men's room and was dead. He was coming home, all right, but he just hadn't said how.

"He was a thirty-third-degree Mason, and all the family gathered for a full Masonic funeral.

"After John's death, there was no place for me in Belle's life. She wrote to my Cousin Martha that I should be sent to an Episcopal orphanage. Instead, Cousin Martha arranged for me to go live with my father's brother in South Lancaster, Massachusetts. I was sent there just like a loaf of bread.

"Uncle Edwin came down in an old jalopy and drove me back to his house. It was a terrible place. The worst slum. They called it the Beehive. Most of the people who lived there were French Canadians. They were all losers. Life was beyond belief. Dumps in the back of the houses. No heating. No sheets on the beds. Only an old army blanket.

"Once I asked my Aunt Cerity why they didn't have any sheets on the beds and she said that it was because sheets were too cold. There was hardly any food. They had a tin tub in the kitchen.

"Uncle Edwin was a dear sweet man, but he was shiftless. Aunt Cerity knew I was miserable, so she wrote to Cousin Martha. After a few months, Cousin Martha arranged for me to live with Uncle Rob and Sue."

We went on talking for a while. Then I asked her about her oldest sister. I had never suspected that she had another sister until my Aunt Irma had told me a few years before about her existence. I was all the more surprised that my mother had never told me, because her sister's name had turned out to be the same as that of the woman I was once married to. Virginia.

"She died a year after Mama. She was so beautiful. She died of consumption. She took such a long time to die. I was still living with Aunt Belle at the time. She forced me to go to the hospital twice each week to visit Virginia. She literally died right in front of my eyes. Each week she would get thinner and thinner. Her skin became almost translucent.

"Aunt Belle was always telling me that I would get TB too, because I had been exposed. She scared the devil out of me. I worried myself sick seeing what it did to my sister. When Virginia finally died, she weighed only twenty-four pounds, and she was sixteen years old.

"I simply refused to admit that she had died or that she had even existed. I guess I went a little crazy. They forced me to go to the funeral against my will. For months afterward, they made me wear a black armband.

"I've never talked to anyone about it until just now. I just couldn't do it."

My mother started to cry, and tears began to gush out of my eyes too.

"Of course, you couldn't have told anyone. How could you have? There had been too many deaths."

I saw her weeping through my own tears and everything seemed to be turning damp and soggy around us.

It was the first time I could ever remember weeping with my mother.

Before I left their house, I went into my mother's bedroom. Everything else in the house, all the other rooms, had been so carefully prepared to be seen. Cleaned, mended, brushed, polished. It is only this room, where only she goes, that has been allowed to deteriorate. Garments thrown on the chaise longue. Her body shape still clinging to them. Odor of tears. Water-stained wallpaper falling away from the plaster in tattered streamers.

The old things that have been there for so long. Ever since I can remember. A dresser, the bed. Already they seem like relics. Everything so neglected and uncared for.

Walking into the room is like walking into my mother's secret sense of herself.

Last night I dreamt that I entered my grandmother's house. It was much smaller than I had imagined it to be. But still it was very grand. I felt very good that she had let me come into her house and stay, even though it had been made clear that she wasn't going to leave the house to me in her will. I knew I was going to explore the house. Uncover all its secrets. I went from room to room and finally into her bedroom, where there were two rumpled beds. All secrets ultimately lead to unmade beds. The odd thing is that I felt no shame or embarrassment about being there. I thought it was my right to know. That even in that room there was nothing that I had to keep secret. That everything could be told. Everything I could possibly tell.

This morning I sit in the car outside a white wooden frame house hugged by a small half-circle of elms, where my great-aunt lives. I am not in a hurry to go in. I know that once I learn about my past there will be no way I can get rid of it or expunge it. It is so cold that even inside the car my exhalations are like huge plumes of smoke.

I go up to the door and ring the bell. I press it and press it again and wait for some response. And then I remember that I am not in New York, where doors are locked and people press bells to let you in.

I open the door on a long flight of stairs. I see a flashing motion and a rush of light at the top. I yell up "Hello." And a voice answers.

"Is that you, Gregory? You're late. I'd just about given up on you."

I go up the stairs and there she is. Tall and straight. Her face a mass of fine wrinkles. Aquiline nose. A mass of white hair that sits on the top of her head like a pod of cotton.

"I was hoping you would come." She steps back and looks at me, and asks me again as she had on the phone, "And it really is you and not some kind of trick?" As if I would tell her if it was. And she is slightly confused. Not knowing what to do with me because I am such an unexpected presence in her house.

We stand there in wonder of each other. She makes a motion for me to follow her.

"My husband, Arnold, is feeling very poorly today. He is resting. He's going to try to get up a little later to say hello to you."

We walk past an open door. A man is stretched out on a bed. His eyes are open. He has the face of a drowning man. Only his head shows above a sea of white sheets. He gives no sign of recognition, so I don't speak. I have been sick too, so I know how much energy it can cost sometimes just to recognize another human being when you are weak.

Ina and I go into the living room. And since we are very close to each other, I put my arms around her. She is unprepared for my embrace. Her body is almost totally still. There is nothing yielding or soft about it. And yet she doesn't resist me. I can feel her wanting to give way but not trusting herself. Her body gives off no energy or warmth. It is almost like embracing a tree.

Finally I let her go and there is a dampness in her eyes. She stands off and looks at me again.

"Not much of Al Andrews in you, but I can see some of Florence." Her voice is very businesslike, almost clipped. She motions me to sit down. "I don't think that hardly a day has passed since it happened that I haven't prayed for this moment. I feel that God has answered my prayers."

And she says these awesome words with no emotion whatsoever. She enunciates them like a mother duck hustling all her young into proper order, fussily nudging them with her beak, not tolerating even the slightest hint of independence.

"Now tell me how you found us. . . ."

I tell her how I tracked her down through a maze of old records.

"I was just ten years old when it happened. I often think of that day when the twins were given away. It was one of the greatest tragedies of my life. I would have given anything to keep them if I could have. If only I could have been a few years older." She perches on the couch almost as weightlessly as a parakeet.

"I remember saying to my mother, 'Why can't we keep them?' But there was no way we could afford to." Another silence as she reaches back into her memory. "Florence, your grandmother, should have never gotten married and she should never have had any children." There is a trace of bitterness in her voice.

"How did they get married?"

"Well, they had to. Al, your grandfather, was working at a farm down the road. Florence was sixteen years old. She used to go down to milk the cows at night. Al came up the road and that was that. When my father found out she was pregnant, they had to get married and that was all there was to it." Ina's voice is so prim and fatalistic. As if to say: *Well, that's the way things happen and there is nothing we can do about it.*

"If Al had been around when my father found out, he would have killed him. It never should have happened. It was a piece of carelessness. After they got married, she went down to live in Al's cabin."

"Was Al a lady's man?"

"Well, if he was, it's the first time I've heard of it."

"Was he handsome?"

"I suppose some people might say so. I never thought he was much. Al was dark and he had regular sort of features. I suppose you could say he was a nice-looking fellow. One thing was certain, though; hard work never did agree with him. He had a way of always showing up at mealtimes. Never talked much. A real quiet sort of fellow. But he would not work and he would not get a job. He made no effort to support the children. No one could make him either. In the winter, Florence would usually go back to live with Mother. In the summer, she would go back to live with Al. In the spring another baby would be born. They spent one winter together in Al's cabin after the twins were born. The twins used to sleep outside in a small shack. It would get so cold out there that a bucket of water would freeze solid in a few minutes. One night my father went down there and found the twins crying. They had wet themselves and their clothing was frozen stiff as a board. Al and Florence had a fire going inside the cabin and it was warm as toast. And my father said that if there was any heat the twins should have it, and if he ever found the twins out in that shack in the cold he would kill Al. I was just learning to bake bread. I'd sit the twins at the table and give them dough to play with. Cecil was my favorite. He was the real lively one. Always asking me questions and following me around wherever I went. Cecil was a little bigger because he was the first born. Do you know which one was your father?"

"I seem to remember that he was Cecil." Actually, there is no sure way I could know which twin my father was, but I want him to have been the favorite. I haven't come all this way to learn that even his own aunt preferred his brother.

But Ina must have heard the uncertainty in my voice. She gives me another chance to tell the truth.

"Cecil was bigger."

And then I tell an outright lie. "I think my father was always the bigger one." But I don't know anything of the sort. I think of my father the way I have known him over the years, his endless silences, the rage which covered him like a skin of ice, his brooding bitterness. I know he must have been Harold, the one who made himself hard to know, because Ronald, his brother, was still a loving ingratiating boy when I knew him so many years later. But I won't admit it to Ina.

I think back to the time that Ronald came to spend a few days with us when I was in grammar school. He slept in my room and

I slept on the couch in the living room. I remember waking up in the morning as he came into the living room and he was my father, but his face was so soft and dreamy. I knew I didn't have to be afraid of him and that I could be myself with him.

I remember that morning as if it were a miracle. The sun was just coming in the window. I could never remember waking up in sunlight before, because my room was in the back where only varying shades of darkness ever penetrated. The white sheets all around me were crumpled into hills and valleys, and the sun's rays ignited them into darting fingers of fire. When my father entered the room just a few seconds later, I couldn't even look at him. It was as if a cloud had suddenly covered the sun. I remember hoping that some mistake had been made and that Ronald was really my father. Even thinking in my half-sleep that perhaps they could get confused and Ronald would stay and my father would leave.

To exculpate myself for lying, I bring out the photo of my father and his brother taken nine months after I was born. They are sitting together on the steps of their foster mother's mansion with me perched on my father's knee.

"Which one is your father?"

I point to the austere man with the mustache and the rimless glasses, who has hidden himself so completely from the world. And the other man, his brother, seems almost completely naked in his beauty, smooth cheeked and open eyed.

"Harold was very handsome." And from the tone of her voice I realize that she knows about my deception. "What happened to him?" There is a very special apprehension and tenderness in her voice.

"He died in Portland in 1948." For a few minutes we both mourn him with our silence.

"What did he die of?" Very aware of dying and the imminence of death. At eighty-one, it is a question which must be very familiar to her lips.

"A heart attack. When he was a boy, he had rheumatic fever and his heart became enlarged." And I remember my mother telling me how everyone was so cruel to Ronald, always calling him lazy and blaming him for not working and for sponging off his foster mother, when all the time it was his enlarged heart. It is all there in that photo. That soft dreaminess that always seems to signify an early death, that unmarked face that never entered the world of men or work, that never really aged or was able to sink roots very firmly into the earth. And there is my father beside him, hanging on for dear life, digging into life with a vengeance.

"And he died right here in Portland, just a few miles away. And he never came up here."

"I'm sure he didn't know. Once he was supposed to have talked about trying to find out who his real mother was, but I don't think he ever did anything about it."

"To think he was so close and we never knew anything about it." And for a few minutes we are both silent, suffused with the wonder of all the people who have been so close to us and yet who have passed by us unnoticed.

I think back to the time when my father's twin brother died. I was eighteen. As with everything else in his life, my father allowed me no part in his brother's death. We never spoke about it together. We never even acknowledged that his brother who was so much like himself had died. As with everything else in his life, my father experienced the death of his brother alone.

He was the only mourner at his brother's funeral. He dressed his brother in his own clothes. The burial was held in the rain. Dressed in his brother's clothes, my father drove his brother's dilapidated truck back to Connecticut stuffed with all his brother's belongings. Piece by piece, my mother threw out Ronald's clothes. After months of badgering, she finally forced him to sell his brother's truck.

Ina breaks the silence by asking about my father's health, her voice telling me how close we all are to death. I tell her about my father's heart attack and his emphysema and how sometimes, when he's tired, I can hear him wheezing and whistling. Ina's face becomes solemn and mournful.

"Is his wife still alive?" I describe my mother's health, how she can't leave the house anymore, and then show her a photo of my mother, standing in the backyard of our old house holding a small milk-white infant in her arms. I stand beside her, a seven-year-old

38

malcontent, burrowing morosely into myself because she is holding my brother, looking angrily down at my tattered sneakers so no one can tell what I am feeling. And my mother looks as if she is appealing to some unseen God to take her but to leave her children.

"Your mother is very beautiful. Cecil was lucky. And is that you?" Pointing to the sullen gargoyle by my mother's side.

"Yes. My father cooks all the meals and does all the housework now."

"She's very lucky he still can take care of her. Arnold, my husband"—her voice very clearly marks her sense of his separateness —"I couldn't get along without him. He goes to the store for me and helps out around the house. And he's not very strong, you know. Just a couple of months ago he slipped and fell, and he's still not really well. Sometimes when he goes to the store, the wind is so strong. It goes right through him, even though he wears a vest and a scarf."

And as I listen to her, I realize that all those things that are taken for granted for so many years—a trip to the store—become perilous adventures again in old age, just the way they are when you are a child.

"He should be getting up soon and then we can have dinner."

I ask her if she will help me with the family tree I have been trying to work out. I take out the ledger book where I have started to trace the roots of my past, which now looks like a hieroglyphic track of termite channels across the paper, the code of life itself, the DNA of my being.

I hold up the book between us because she couldn't possibly read my almost illegible scrawl. I read the names off to her.

"You've done a lot of work already."

And I glow because I am sitting so close to my grandmother's sister. Soon the page is almost black with names.

"Andrew Kincaid came from Vermont and was married to Ida Maxwell of Whitefield, who was the daughter of James Maxwell and Aurora Bloggett.

"He had four daughters and a son. Florence—she was the oldest. Then there came me, then Mildred and last Bessie. Ike was born after Florence. He was named after his father's brother. He married an Elizabeth Maxwell, no relation to his mother. His son Michael married the woman you talked to on the phone.

"Hernando was Florence's oldest son. He got married and had five children. The oldest was also named Ike. Hernando was very close to my brother. His middle name is not Albourne as you've got it here, but Albert after his father. I think she got his first name from one of her teachers. Florence also had two daughters, Ada and Reena. One of Ada's daughters may be coming down after lunch."

I write everything down as fast as I can because it seems as if I will never have another chance like this. Because Ina seems so tensely and tenuously a part of life. It seems as if the cord that binds her to this world could snap at any time.

After a while there is a sound of shuffling outside the door.

"I think that must be Arnold."

We both get up to receive him. The door opens and a tall wisp of a man like the broken branch of a tree after a storm enters the room. His face is almost as transparent as water. His eyes are unutterably sad. His shoes seem to be as big as a Keystone Kop's, and his nose is spread all over his face like a limp cucumber.

Ina introduces me to him as Cecil's son.

"Very glad to meet you." His voice has the quality of an old recording played at a very slow speed. Ina shows him the family tree and he glances at it briefly with his huge sad eyes.

"That's nice." But he doesn't even look at it because he seems tremendously wary of any sudden demands on his waning energy. All he wants to do is to get into the kitchen without any mishap.

Soon they are both at work preparing dinner. Arnold takes the butter and bread and fruit from the icebox. Ina tends the pots. They handle food almost as if it were part of a religious ceremony. Their food is so precious to them now because there are so many things they can't eat anymore. Ina tells me very seriously about how various foods affect them both. She can't eat salad because it gives her heartburn. She had a piece of pie yesterday and it didn't bother her. So she is going to try another piece today, but she is very wary. She loves stewed tomatoes, but they have too much acid.

I realize that food is one of their last links to the world of the living. Each year it becomes harder to eat, harder to swallow, harder to digest, harder to live with the consequences of eating. Each year there are fewer and fewer things they can eat. They measure their waning life expectancy by the kinds of food they are still able to digest. So each morsel is precious to them. They pray to their food the way men pray to anything that seems to hold their fates so capriciously.

Ina heaps my plate with food as if I am expected to eat for them both as well. And though I have eaten breakfast only a couple of hours ago, I find that I am very hungry. Their famished looks somehow whet my appetite. Ina tells her husband what I am doing and he tries to seem interested. But soon they have forgotten about me and are talking about what really concerns them, the failing health of their friends.

When we finish, they make it very clear that I am not to help. They have their ways and they don't like them to be disturbed. I could put something in the wrong place and it could be lost forever. Because all the good intentions in the world wouldn't prevent me from misplacing the butter, and that might be just what would save them.

When they are finished putting things away, I offer to do the dishes. Ina informs me with unmistakable emphasis that Arnold does the dishes. I realize that it too is a precious task, that it is part of the work of the living and that it is a tremendous privilege to still be allowed to live and to do the work of the living.

I know that it is time for me to go. Ina's face is ashen with exhaustion. I take her in my arms. Her body is as firm and unyielding as a mannequin's.

"You look so tired. I know you've got to take a nap."

There is a mistiness in her eyes, but I know she won't let herself cry in front of me.

"When can I see you again?"

She asks me to supper and I demur. But I promise to come

afterward and stay until their bedtime. She makes me promise I won't forget and chides me for being late this morning.

"I almost didn't think you were coming." I know she doesn't want to let me go. I know that she is trying to think of some way to keep me, even though she is dropping in her tracks.

"I feel as if God has sent you in answer to my prayer."

She walks me to the door, past the room where Arnold is stretched out napping in his clothing on a small bed. Ina stands watching me as I descend the staircase and go out into the street.

After supper I go back and ring the bell. A light goes on and the staircase is suddenly illuminated. Ina is all aglow. Callers in the evening must be very rare. She takes me into the kitchen and gives me a piece of pie. Like a mother now. I can tell that she has been thinking about me and worrying about me. She has decided to take care of me and treat me as a real grandson and not just a miraculous stranger.

"I've been thinking and trying to get things straight in my head. It's been so long. You see, I don't think Florence ever had any feeling for her children. When you come right down to it, I doubt if she had much feeling for anyone. The only time anyone could ever remember her crying was the day the twins left. Even then it wasn't really crying. Her eyes just sort of got wet. Even after she died, she had a mean expression on her face.

"Flo was a tomboy. She couldn't keep any clothes on. She loved horses. Loved to climb trees. She always had to have the best. The best dog. The best horse. Had no shame about what she said in front of the boys. Always embarrassed her brother, Ike. She would talk indecently right out in front of a crowd of men. Ike dreaded to see her coming.

"She paid no attention to the younger children. She was a law unto herself. Our mother used to say she could never do anything with Flo.

"She would go to the livery stable and hire horses and drive them near to death. She always thought she was better than anyone else. She loved to see other people getting a beating. She'd break the sticks for Mother.

42

"After she divorced Al, she married John Hamlin. He was a good man. He had a good job, even though he drank. Florence never should have left him. She never did have much luck with men.

"After she left him she had to get a job in a mill. Then she got married a third time, to a guy named Clinton Swain. I don't know where she picked him up. The sorriest excuse for a human being you ever did see. He claimed to be some kind of retired engineer. He was an old epileptic millhand and a drunk to boot. I know he was always having fits. Most of the time, Florence had to support him. It wasn't long after that when she married Reuben Kelley, the homeliest man I ever met. Then she divorced him and married Eli Stukey. She divorced him and then married him again. All I can remember about him is that he used to drink strained canned heat.

"Altogether Florence had five children, including the twins—Hernando, Cecil, Harold, Ada and Reena—and she gave up every one of them for adoption."

"Do you know anything else about my grandfather?"

"Well, not really, I never spent much time with him. He was a quiet sort. I seem to remember that he spent some time in the reformatory in South Windham before he came up to Arbor."

I draw a deep breath. So there is no end to what I will have to learn to accept. I ask her about Mamie Lynn, my grandfather's second wife.

"Well, she was one of the queerest ducks you ever saw. She had an eye in her head that would kill you. I was never able to make up my mind about whether she was as ugly as she seemed. She was from Lynnville. The Lynns were the next thing to dogs. They'd married and intermarried until they were all morons. I remember how she and Al would sometimes go round looking for farm work. They always had a can of pea soup."

It is too much, more than my mind can bear. I suppose it is the worst story I have ever heard. And now I will have to live with it because it is mine.

I can hardly get up from my chair to leave. Ina is starting to fall asleep right in front of my eyes. I leave abruptly and ungraciously because I can no longer bear to stay in that room.

43

Afterward I head back to my motel, as if its sterility would be some kind of refuge. I have gotten so much more than I ever expected. My mind refuses to absorb it. It is as if there were a dam somewhere inside my head. The past backs up and floods me. I say to myself that I don't want to see Ina again, but I know they are only idle words. Now that I have found her, I will never let her go.

And yet, I don't want the past that she has given me. It wasn't what I came here to find.

I am too restless to stay in my room, so I go out to the lobby. I ask the room clerk about the town, and he tells me that "the joint is really jumping." I ask him where, and with one of those looks of arch complicity that pass between men at such times, he tells me about a place down the road. "They tell me you can get anything you want down there."

Outside the snow is glistening white in the streets. I drive back and forth looking for the place. Finally I decide that it must be a roadhouse hotel about four blocks away. I park and follow the sound of the music to a large, dimly lit room with a bar at one end, a three-piece orchestra and people dancing. There are only couples and groups of people.

I order a beer and fall into conversation with the barmaid. I try to explain to her what I am doing in Maine. She seems interested for a while and then her attention wanes. She dances over to the other end of the bar and stands there making drinks, twirling the glasses in the air like pompons, wiggling and grinding her body to the music. After a while my eyes accustom themselves to the darkness, and I watch the people dancing. They are all keyed up. Working people, determined to have a good time and get their money's worth. Their pale faces are almost phosphorescent under the artificial light. The men command the waitresses to their tables with gestures of largess, very much aware of the exercise of their power. Yet when they dance, the men are all so awkward and wooden. And I wonder what they have done to men like myself in this country so they can't dance. Can't let themselves go. But the women are so different. They flaunt their abandon and rapture

44

so tauntingly. But the men can't let themselves be enticed out of themselves because they might seem ridiculous. Because to a man, beauty of self has been made to seem so perilously close to shame. So they hide their beauty and grace behind their awkward exhaustion.

And I sit there watching them for what seems like hours. And later, some single women appear at the bar. They look at me, but I am too tired to move from my chair and speak to them. I can't even smile.

That night in my room, I dream about crossing bridges over endless chasms. Watching helplessly as they crumble around me and shards of debris tumble against my falling body. And those dreams are replaced by dreams of falling into old abandoned mine shafts, debris of old shoring raining against my body.

And even in my dreams I know that it is just my sense of myself that is crumbling around me and that I am really tumbling helplessly into the past. That I have lost the ground that was underneath my feet, and that I have no idea where I will finally land or if I will ever land.

$$\overline{\underline{}}$$

Ina is waiting for me when I arrive the next day. She has gone through all her old boxes of memorabilia and found photos of her sisters, Mildred and Bessie, whom I'll be meeting soon, and a number of photos of herself at various stages of her life. She has also found a lock of her hair dating back to the time she was a young girl.

She hasn't been able to sleep the night before because I've stirred up so many old memories. But she is very "chipper." My coming has given her "a whole new lease on life." Her eye is sharper and her back even straighter. Perched on the edge of her couch, she is like a very proud, beautiful girl waiting to be asked to dance. And she wants very much to tell me all about herself.

Yet she is not really sure I want to hear. It is really her own past that she wants to remember with me. She wants me to understand that she is a person too, in her own right. She explains how she

45

went to live in Washington, D.C., with her first husband, who was a guard at the National Gallery. And how she used to spend days on end looking at the paintings. I can feel the fullness as the past rises up so palpably inside her.

And she smiles apologetically, as if to say: *I know I am boring you, but it is so important to me to remember and to be able to tell you, because I'm sure you will understand.* Her young girlishness sweeps away all the marks of age. And it is almost as if we were in a grove of cherry trees and she were wearing a big straw hat with a streamer and a long flowing dress. I feel as if we should put on a phonograph record and dance away all the vestiges and accretions of age and mustiness that have accumulated in that room over the years. As if her antiquity were simply a disguise that she could remove at will. Dance away the years. I know she feels this too because, even though she never met me before this trip, I am still a creature of her youth. My presence brings back to life so many girlish dreams. She is eighty-one years old and she is still a girl.

After they left Washington, they moved back to Maine, to North Vassalboro. And when she mentions the name, a mistiness comes into her eyes.

"It was just a summer cottage, but we fixed it up real nice. It was good to come back to Maine because we missed it so terribly much." There is a faint tremolo in her voice as she shows me a photo of her house. Then she shows me a photo of herself standing many years ago on a small bridge festooned with bowers of flowers. I ask her if Florence ever came to visit.

"No. Florence wasn't much of a one for visiting."

Her answer is tense and hurried, as if she hadn't really wanted the name of her sister in her mouth. I can almost see her lips puckering. I know it was the wrong question to ask, but sometimes I am tactless.

"Florence and I never had very much to say to each other. She sent me a birthday card once. I'll try to find it for you. Toward the end, when I knew she was having a hard time, I used to send her money once in a while, but we were never really close." She looks up at me and squints.

"You know, I could never have any children of my own. I had a growth, which had to be removed."

She doesn't have to say it. We both know now. Florence gave away the twins and it was like giving away Ina's own children. The children Ina could never have. Now I know why she said the other day that having the twins leave was one of the greatest tragedies of her life. Now I understand.

"Why didn't your father take Florence's children?" I ask. Ina pulls back from her reverie. Her body jerks.

"Well, Ada came to live with us for a while. I think Florence and the kids lived in the attic for a while once, but something happened and they had to move out." For the first time, I get a definite sense that Ina is hiding something from me.

"How did they live?"

"Sometimes neighbors would give them milk and vegetables. For a while they used to get help from the state. Then Albert Miller—he was the selectman—made them go to the poor farm. He said the town wouldn't give them any more money unless Florence worked for it. Miller was the one who forced her to give up the twins. Of course, no man can make you give up your children if you want to keep them. Miller was the one who took the twins down to Boston with my mother to the Little Wanderers Orphanage."

I've had enough now. I have to go now.

"You look very tired. I'm going to leave now. But I'd like to see Bessie and Mildred."

"I've already talked to them. They both want to see you. Millie wants to have her hair fixed first. She has the most beautiful long white hair you have ever seen. She wants you to come out day after tomorrow. I told her that it would be very hard for her not to think about you as if you were one of the twins, because I was always getting confused today myself. Bessie wants to see you too. She's out in Vienna. It will take you all day to get there and back. I'll have to give you some directions because there has been a lot of flooding and some of the roads have been washed out."

Ina stands very close to me. And there is such a look of love in her eyes that I almost find myself melting.

47

"I thank the Lord for the gift of you. Am I going to see you tomorrow?"

I tell her that I will come back again next morning. The door of Arnold's room is closed. Ina stands at the head of the stairs and watches me out the door as if she expected me never to return.

⩡

The next time I saw her my mother described her marriage.

"We set up housekeeping in a one-room apartment with a folding bed, a little kitchen and a dinette. A friend of your father's gave us some silver. I made a cover for the bed.

"I would spend the days cleaning. I'd have my coat and hat on every night, waiting for your father to come home to take me to the movies. One day I discovered an entry in your father's notebook that he had probably left open for me to see.

"It said: 'I hate going out to dinner. I'm so hungry for a home-cooked meal.'

"Your father's stepsister, Ellen, showed me how to cook lamb chops, baked potato and cake. When your father came home, dinner was waiting for him and there were candles on the table.

"Your father hated the movies. I could never forgive him because one night he laughed at *Anna Karenina* with Greta Garbo and John Gilbert. There was only one exception to the way he felt about movies. Clive Brook was your father's favorite. Any time I'd mention Clive Brook, your father would have his hat on, ready to go.

"Our apartment was over a nightclub, The Green Parrot. Once we went away for a weekend. When we returned, we found some men in the apartment drinking and playing cards. I screamed. Your father lost his temper. I got so scared for him. The men looked so tough I thought they might hurt him. It turned out the superintendent had let the men in the apartment to play cards for the weekend.

"A short time after we came down here to Connecticut, the crash hit. Your father's foster mother lost all her money. Ten million dollars.

"First your father's twin brother came to live with us. He

couldn't hold a job. Every time he'd get something, he'd be fired within a week. Once Pop got him a job where he worked. Pop's boss didn't want to hire him because he said the idea of having twins around gave him the jitters. Ronald was supposed to go to work earlier than Pop. But he always went in with Pop. That was the reason he got fired. Pop was furious. He thought Ron was just lazy. We didn't know it at the time, but he had rheumatic fever when he was sixteen, and he had gotten an enlarged heart. It was that that finally killed him. When he was living with us, he had no drive or ambition. You felt like giving him a good boot. I felt sorry for him. He seemed like a broken man. He had always depended on his foster mother's money and now there was none. It seemed like such an effort for him even to get out of his chair.

"Once when he got really discouraged, he ran out of the house with his gun. It was teeming rain. Pop ran after him. I was scared to death. They both stayed out for hours. Neither of them wore a hat. When they came back, they were both drenched. It turned out they had been sitting on a railway bridge talking all that time. They were much closer after that.

"My sister Irma was living with another aunt of mine at the time. But something happened and she had to leave. One afternoon Aunt Lottie just drove up with Irma and put her off at our house with her suitcase. What were we to do? She had no money and nowhere else to go. Pop was furious. Here we didn't have very much money and Pop was supporting my sister and his own brother.

"After you were born, you slept in the same room with Ronald."

Those few tantalizing fragments, those few suggestive bits of information that I would sometimes hear about my father, would reverberate endlessly in my mind. My mother used to say that he had been a racing car driver. It turned out that he had driven in a few races on dirt tracks and quit after he had an accident and broke a leg.

My mother, so hungry for images of my father's strength and power and social prestige, used to say that he had gone to college at Brown, where he had been a halfback on the football team. The truth of the matter was that he had never gone to college at all. Instead, once he had been sent away for a year to a prep school named Moses Brown.

I remember how she used to press him to affirm her dreams. Her face glowing with the depth of her need to poeticize him.

"You played football, didn't you, Matt?"

No matter what he would say or how he would qualify her assertion, she would go on as if he had completely affirmed what she had said. Finally he would regard her with a blank stare, as if to say: *All right. Go ahead and believe anything you want to because I know there isn't anything I can do to prevent you.*

How my mother used to nourish herself on her dreams of his foster mother's great wealth. How many times didn't I hear how we had been cheated out of a proper share of her vast fortune. The few relics we did inherit were treated like holy objects. The kidney-shaped desk. The Iranian bronze coffee table. The oriental rug.

There was my father. Solitary. Angry. Forbidding. My mother tried to superimpose these objects on her perception of him like a trompe l'oeil painting. To see him through the shimmering film of their magnificence. Out of a few shreds of history she had to create a whole man. A husband.

Sometimes she attempted to paint him as a great Romeo. She used to tell the same story over and over again about the love affair he had had with a girl before his marriage to her. She would go on about the great delight he took in combing this woman's long golden hair. My father would nod. He had never touched another woman before or after my mother. Yet somehow this romance made him seem more real to my mother. Later on she used to pretend that he was having a clandestine affair with someone in his office. She would cluck over this imaginary romance like a mother hen. Pleased as punch. My father would regard her with stony silence.

My mother always used to tell me that when she first met him, he was driving a Stutz Bearcat, wearing a raccoon coat and a derby. I don't know how many times I heard that story. It is etched deeply in my mind through innumerable repetitions. And yet, talking to them recently, I discovered a different truth. He didn't have the raccoon coat until after they got married. She had made him buy it to conform to her image of what the man she married had to be. Then she simply went ahead and convinced herself that he had had it all along. For years it hung in our closet as tangible proof of her imagination of his magnificence when he married her. I used to sneak out of the house with it on sometimes, reliving my mother's dream of my father.

But it wasn't my father at all. It had nothing to do with his own sense of himself. He didn't buy the coat. She simply dressed him in her dreams. At the same time she made him buy the coat, she also made him buy a pair of square-toed shoes because they were the chic mode of all the seniors in her high school class.

How much of his reality ever got through to her? She never allowed herself to know her husband as he really was. Instead, she chose to live in the loneliness of dreams.

⤇

I haven't been at Ina's for more than a few minutes when the doorbell rings.

"That must be Carolyn Steiner, Ada's daughter, your first cousin. When I told her you were coming, she wanted to see you so much."

Carolyn is blond and faintly Scandinavian. She smiles almost frantically at Ina, like a glass that knows it is falling to the floor and that it is only a matter of seconds until it will be a thousand splinters. For some reason, she can't bring herself to look at me directly. Even when she talks to me, she still looks at Ina.

"You must have been really amazed when you heard from him."

"I couldn't believe it. I asked him if it was a trick."

And I can still hear in Ina's voice a faint residue of her suspicion that I am some kind of devious confidence man. Her voice also warns me unmistakably to remain the miracle that I am supposed to be.

"Ina has never stopped talking about the twins. I never could understand how anyone could give away two such beautiful boys." She gets that look on her face people get when they know they are about to say something awful. "Florence has always reminded me of that woman who killed her three children and was put in the insane asylum. When she got out, she got married again and had three more children. She drowned them all and then threw herself in the river."

And I think of the strands of silver hair I had seen swirling in the Kennebec River on my first night in Maine. And in spite of the traces of horror that I hear in my cousin's voice, I also detect a kind of envy. I think to myself that all women somewhere inside themselves must want to be like my grandmother and throw off all their children and abandon the yoke of maternity. That all women somewhere just want to be free.

I take out my pictures and show them to Carolyn. Ina leaves the room to search for some photos of her own. Carolyn's eyes unerringly light on my uncle.

"Oh, isn't he handsome. Is he your father?" When I point out my father, she grudgingly admits that he is handsome too.

Ina has found a photo of my great-grandmother. She is plump and bemused and solemn. Blond curls peep out from under what seems to be a velvet cap. She looks as if she could have come straight out of a Rembrandt painting. And all of us in this room have somehow emerged from her loins.

"My mother was a very beautiful woman. She never said a harsh word to anyone." And then Ina hands me a photo of my great-grandfather. A Rembrandt too. "He was a hard man." Ferrety eyes. Stubborn. Strong-willed. Utterly insensitive to others. A man who would hold a grudge forever. But oddly beautiful in his stubborn, strong-willed pride.

"Would you like to see a photo of your grandmother?" She passes me a photo of three women. "Can you tell which one is your grandmother?"

One of them is very modish and feminine. Another is very beautiful and intense. The third is handsome like a man. Large squarish face. Short blond hair. Large body. Her eyes stare out from the photo with the nullity of schizophrenia. The other two women are very conscious of projecting their beauty and character for the posterity of the camera. But the third woman doesn't seem the least bit aware of being photographed. And yet she dominates the photo. I find my eyes drawn back to her again and again. She could almost be a man in disguise. Her impassivity is terrifying.

"Can you tell?"

I shake my head, not wanting to make a mistake and identify the wrong woman as my grandmother.

"Well. That's my friend." Pointing to the pretty, almost Gainsboroughesque woman in the gathered velvet shirt. "That's me in the center." The somber beauty. "And that's Florence." Pointing to the face which is like stone. I look again, and I get a sense of a woman who is lost almost completely inside herself. I can almost see her dreams like a seething hive behind her eyes. And I am stunned into silence because I see something of my own expression in her bitter withdrawal.

I look up from the photo and there are Carolyn's eyes staring at me apprehensively. We both wince at the same time. Neither of us willing to acknowledge the intensity of her stare. And I have a sense that I frighten her. And I guess that it is all the things that still haven't been said.

"Are there any photos of my grandfather?"

Carolyn answers that she thinks she has one somewhere and that she will look for it.

"I also remember a beautiful picture of the twins dressed in some kind of sailor suits. Do you have that one, Ina?"

"I know which one you mean, but I can't remember if I have it." They go on to talk about a woman who bought Florence's house after she died. The photo was in the attic but the woman wouldn't let anyone in the house.

"That was the most heartbreaking photo I think I've ever seen. It was taken the day the twins left for the Little Wanderers home. Hernando is standing in the middle holding the twins' hands. He was three years older. The twins were wearing Russian sailor suits. I don't know where they got them from. Cecil was twirling a button and Harold was completely unconcerned. I'll never forget that day. It was worse than a funeral." As she remembers, there is a catch in her throat. "I've thought of that day again and again and I still can't understand how she could do such a thing."

For a few minutes we all stop to relive that day in our imagination. Carolyn breaks the silence.

"You know, I've got to get back to work now." I can sense the relief in her voice, at having an excuse to leave. "I really want to have you out to dinner." Still not looking at me. "But we'll have to wait until I come into town again next week. I don't think you could ever find your way out yourself. What with the snow, and all the flooding, it's almost impossible to drive. This one hill is so steep that you have got to build up a lot of speed before you start up or you can never make it. The bottom is covered with ice. Just before you get to that spot, the road is almost completely washed out." As she goes on elaborating the dangers of the trip, I realize that I will never be invited to Carolyn's.

I don't know what I have done or said, or what I remind her of. But I know that it isn't just the dangers of the trip she is describing, but the tremendous danger she senses of having me in her house.

⇟

Before I came up to Maine, I got my mother to tell me what she knew about my father's early childhood.

He was sent to the Little Wanderers Orphanage in Boston with his brother when they were two and a half. A year later they were both taken to live with an English couple in Florida. The woman actually wrote children's books about the twins which were published as *The Reggie and Roger Stories*. The family broke up after a year and the twins were returned to the orphanage.

The orphanage doctor was also the doctor for a very wealthy lady whose husband had died a short time before. He told her all about the twins. How beautiful they were and how unhappy. How he didn't want to break them up but no one seemed to want to adopt them together. She is supposed to have replied, "I'd love to see them. Bring them out for a weekend."

They never went back to the orphanage again. After the first day at her mansion, my father is supposed to have remarked, "I like this hotel. Can we stay?"

He was used to hotels because the orphanage would ship its

wards around to various hotels in adjoining states to display them for possible adoption.

In answer to his question, Mrs. Armstrong told him that he and his brother could spend the night. The night stretched into days and weeks and years. Always with the explicit understanding that, if they didn't behave themselves, they would have to go back to the orphanage.

⏝

How my mother loves to talk about the Armstrong household. The two cars. The $6,000 Peerless and the $10,000 Pierce Arrow with the two bodies. All the servants. William Wells, the gardener. Katie Gollar, the nursemaid. Mamie Harrinton, the laundress. Nora, the upstairs maid, who drank. Marie MacNamie, the downstairs maid, who took care of her priest cousin in her spare hours.

That household is the reason why my mother wanted me to be a writer. I was supposed to write about the Armstrong family. The most fascinating story my mother had ever heard. The most beguiling dream she was ever able to dream. The dream that she tried to pass on to me.

Even now she can't imagine why I would want to write about her and her childhood in preference to the story of the Armstrongs. The S. S. Pierce canned goods. The beautiful twins in perfect lace dresses. Guarnerius violins that Mrs. Armstrong gave to her protégés. Fritz Kreisler and musicales. High teas on Sunday. Grand old ladies.

I'd tell the story, but it is really my mother's story. She is the only one who could tell it with the feeling it deserves. The sumptuous accents. Because the only way to tell that story is with the yearning of a teenage orphan girl who has been dreaming it all her life.

I don't think that my mother ever quite forgave my father for turning out not to be rich. Her cousin Valerie must have told her all about his money before she had gone out with him that night. My father was supposed to be a catch. That was what she needed him to be.

His foster mother's money was real enough. But my father had already rejected it before he married my mother, because he felt so rejected by his foster mother. And when my mother finally realized that this was what he had done, all she could see was that my father was a great fool and that he had cheated her of everything she had ever wanted from life. It was as if he had deliberately broken the bones of her dream.

I remember hearing them talk about the effects of his foster mother's sudden loss of fortune.

My mother said with a gloating air, "But at least you got an insurance policy out of it, didn't you, Matt?"

My father corrected her. "Oh, no. You remember, Martha. I cashed it in and gave the money back to her because she needed it after she lost everything in the crash."

My mother looked dejectedly down at the floor.

But it wasn't the money itself my mother wanted. They always had enough food. A car. They belonged to a country club. They were even able to buy a house of their own in a snobbish town.

What my mother wanted was the sainthood of wealth that all orphans must dream about. The sense of miraculous restoration of all that she had lost by the sudden acquisition of great fortune. Money as a symbol of the holy grail. Money as mystical redemption. The only way she could conceive of accepting herself was inside a halo of gold.

Recently my mother told me a story about the early days of their marriage. It was when they were living in a one-room apartment with a Murphy folding bed. My father had built a special radio in a cedar chest for a very wealthy man. He took my mother out with him when he delivered it.

Parked in the millionaire's half-moon driveway was a Hispano Suiza with wire wheels and pipes sticking out of the hood.

"What a way to live," my mother said to my father. "Maybe we will strike it rich someday too. No telling. We just might."

They never did strike it rich. Over the next twenty years, my father devised invention after invention. Over and over again, he was defrauded or duped. It was as if he believed that orphans were not allowed any fulfillment.

But the poorer they were, the happier they seemed to be. They spent the Depression living in two-family houses in poor neighbor-hoods. Everybody would get together for Saturday night parties. Most of the women had young children like my mother. Everyone was living on dreams and hopes.

My father was the local Mr. Fix-It. Everyone brought him their broken appliances.

One man built his own car with Pop's help. My father helped another neighbor build a boat in his basement.

During the war, my father finally got together enough money to buy a new house. I'll always remember that big wad of bills he used for a down payment. He never seemed more powerful or happier.

It was my mother's dream come true. Buying a single-family house. Joining the country club.

But the reality was so different from her expectations. It was the end of their social life. The end of their friendships. The beginning of their long loneliness.

No one came to their house anymore. My parents never went out anywhere. Now they hardly go out of the house at all. Victims of the American dream of wealth.

⸙

I went for a walk alone in the woods today, where I thought the old house might have been where Florence and Al lived.

I couldn't have been too far away. I found an ancient abandoned icehouse that was so rotten the walls were almost like moss. Then I walked behind it into an enormous, endless tract of pine trees. The snow was glistening and unmarked. There were some still-warm deer spore, faint coronas of mist rising from the small brown pellets.

For a long time I just stood in the wet silence. Every now and then there would be a faint stirring, as a bird settled in one of the trees and the branch rippled like water. When I walked, the limbs of the trees brushed against me like hanging silk.

I thought to myself that my grandmother and grandfather made love in these woods, probably not so far from where I was standing. My father almost froze to death not too far from here, crystals of urine like Popsickle shards on his shuddering pink baby body.

Back over on the other side of the road in a small clearing is an automobile junk yard. An old tractor, all its metal consumed by time, now just a fragile shell of brown rust. A scattering of abandoned cars as peaceful as pine cones in the snow.

Tonight I called my parents. They are both tired. The sink in the kitchen has been stopped up all week and they have had to wash all their dishes in the bathroom. The problem is that the pipes are all stopped up with the past, clogged with twenty years of grease and debris. All the fine particles of their daily life which they thought were being washed out to sea. Actually they never left the house.

My father has forced a worm, a pipe borer, more than twenty feet into the plumbing and still the lines are not clear. The refuse of two decades has become so impacted. Cleaning it out is hard work for an old man. Lying in cramped, unfamiliar positions. Using muscles to turn off the pipe fittings which haven't been used for years. He can work for only a few minutes at a time and then he has to rest. It is wearing him out and still there is no end in sight. He doesn't feel well. And my mother tells me that they have both spent the week sighing and gasping for breath.

Because she is such an actress, she sighed for me over the phone. One pure tone, one single exhalation of pain almost like a pigeon's coo.

I told my father that I had found out some things. I waited for him to ask me what I had found out, but the question never came.

I thought to myself that perhaps it would be better if I waited until we were together before I revealed to him what I have found out. We talked for a while about the weather in Maine. I hung up with a tremendous sense of duplicity.

Perhaps I will write him a letter.

When I was a child, they would argue over me until late at night. My mother would croon my name like the fall of a dying bird. My father would crush it between his teeth like a nut.

"I always thought Pop was strangling me. Always hanging on too tight. All my life I had been struggling to be free. I thought Pop was too demanding and possessive. I just thought what he needed was tough. He had had a better life than I had had. Why did he have to feel so deprived and put upon?

"There was no way for us to talk. We disagreed on everything from politics to child rearing. Pop would try to get me to share his views. When I wouldn't, he would get mad. I voted for Roosevelt. Pop voted for Hoover.

"I used to get mad at him because he hated Christmas so. He always accused me of spending too much money. Of spending more money than we had.

"Unfortunately you became the big bone of contention between us. Pop always thought I was spoiling you. I thought he was too cruel and too hard.

"I took the doctor's every word for gospel. I was always fussing over you. The house completely revolved around you. Nothing could have prevented me from giving you a bath every day. And having fresh clean clothes for you. I made sure you brushed every tooth in your head. All your dresses were perfectly ironed and folded.

"Pop was always objecting. I just thought he was insensitive."

My mother told my father in the early days of their marriage that, if he ever laid a hand on her, she would leave him.

He never did hit her. In some ways, it was as if he never even touched her.

After a few years she made him sleep in a cot in the corner of the room because she claimed he was too restless. It was the same cot he had slept in as a boy. Later he moved into a separate room. As the years passed, his relationship with her began more and more to resemble his relationship with his foster mother, who never once kissed him. Who never once let him into her bedroom. The limit of her loving was an occasional pat on the head.

I remember the time I went out to visit them when I had separated from my wife. I accused them of many things, among them that they had never been physically demonstrative with each other. I think I even accused them of never making love.

They both looked down at the table. After a while, my father looked up and said, "Martha didn't enjoy that kind of thing and I didn't want to force her."

I never saw them kiss except for a peck on the cheek when he went off to work. The closest I ever saw him get to her were those rare occasions when he would nuzzle his head in her lap.

He was the troll who lived under the bridge and waited to devour us. He lived so much of his life in that badly lit subterranean darkness that, when he was upstairs, he always seemed to be blinking from the unaccustomed daylight.

It was always my mother's house. Never my father's. The only place he existed was downstairs in his basement workshop.

When my father came into the room, she acted as if a dangerous animal had entered our presence. There was a special tension in the air. My mother's voice would become faintly shrill. I could see her body tense. Hear her trying to modulate the fear out of her voice.

Their arguing never seemed to stop.

Sometimes my father would raise a hand to strike her, but it never fell. At least once a week, my father would lose his temper and storm out of the house with a gun, the way his brother had done. But my mother never went after him.

One night she decided that he had played that trick once too often. The next morning she searched the house and found his hiding place. The next time they had a fight and he started to leave, he found that his gun was missing.

He asked my mother where it was. She announced that she had thrown it away.

"How dare you?" he said. "My brother gave me that gun."

"Well," she replied, "I gave it to the garbage man."

"Once when he was ironing one of his shirts (he always said I couldn't do it well enough), I said something about what a terrible job he was doing. And he took the shirt and tore it to shreds. Another time we were out driving, and I said something he didn't like. He took his derby and smashed it through the stick shift and threw it out the window. Another time in Verona, he took a chair and put it through the floor, rug and all. And you remember how he used to break all the dishes."

⇌

Today, my Aunt Ina told me the story of my Uncle Hernando, the brother my father never knew.

"Florence originally sent him away to the orphanage, even before she sent the twins. In fact, he'd been sent down to the same family in Florida that adopted your father for a while. But Nando was too much trouble and they couldn't keep him. They were always trying him out with different families, but either he'd run away or he'd make too much trouble and they'd send him back to the orphanage.

"When he was eight, he just appeared one evening walking up the road. He'd run away from the orphanage and somehow had managed to get home alone, coming up the road in the darkness with a bundle on his shoulder. I don't know how he did it. Boston was over two hundred miles away and this was back in 1907."

Ina sighs and catches her breath.

"When he got back, Florence still didn't want him. I guess she was living with her second husband at the time. So Florence sent him to the county farm."

Suddenly I have to fight to keep back my tears.

"Hernando really resented being sent to the farm. They worked the kids like animals. He used to talk about it all the time when he got older. He resented the fact that Florence never came to visit him even though all the time he was at the poor farm, she was living only two miles away. I don't think he ever forgave her for that. When he was fourteen, he attacked the guy who ran the poor farm with a pitchfork. From then on, he was on his own.

"For a while he was the strong man in the circus. Once, on the Fourth of July, he dressed up in a gorilla suit and picked up a one-hundred-pound bag of grain with his teeth and tossed it over his head.

"When he was sixteen, he asked his mother to sign him into the army. He fought in Europe and was gassed twice.

61

"After the war, when he came home, he tried to get Florence to live with him. He was worried about the way she was living. But she wouldn't have any part of him. He wound up marrying his first wife, Maude Page, a woman who was twice his age. She was homely as a mud fence.

"After he divorced Maude Page, he was living for a while with his sister, Reena. She was married to this guy, Jess Bailey, at the time. He had a daughter named Yvette. She was only sixteen. Well, Nando got her pregnant and he had to marry her. Nando thought Yvette was the most beautiful woman in the world. They went on to have five children.

"But Nando was a hard man. He had no feelings for people. He used to beat his children something horrible. Sometimes he used to beat his wife too, and she was just a girl.

"Once she was having a little party. You know, just some women in for coffee and cake. It was about ten o'clock. Nando came out of the back room and told them it was time to go home. He wasn't kidding. He was very nasty. He just said this is it and stood there waiting for them to leave.

"It's true that his wife hadn't had the best upbringing. Her father was a drunkard. And she had a very weak face. No chin. No real character. She spoiled the children something terrible. I know that when Nando wasn't feeling well, when his lungs were really giving him a lot of trouble, she didn't treat him very well. Once he told Millie that she said to him when he was sick, 'You can just lie in that bed and die, for all I care.'

"I suppose you heard what happened to Hernando?"

I shake my head.

Ina stops to get her emotions under control.

"It all started when his wife, Yvette, started hanging around with this man. He had a sister and a brother. She would take her oldest son, Ike, and they would all go around riding together in the car. Somehow word got back to Nando that they were all going to run away together to Boston.

"His wife should have known better. Nando had a terrible temper and he had been in the army, where he just used to kill and kill and kill. I couldn't blame her, though, for thinking about leaving him.

"When Nando first heard of her affair, he tried to sign himself into the Veterans' Hospital because I guess he knew what he was going to do. But they told him he only had family trouble.

"It was a terrible thing to have happen. You'd have thought there would have been a way to avoid it." Ina turns to me with a very somber look. "He told Millie, my sister, several weeks before that she should look after him and call him up from time to time because he wasn't going to let his wife get away with it. He told Millie that if he couldn't have her, no one else was going to.

"The day it happened, it was sort of warm and foggy. Nando got in his truck with his shotgun and went off looking for this fellow to kill him. He drove around all morning. But he couldn't find him so he went back home. He found his wife in the bathtub.

"Millie had a premonition that something was going to happen. In the afternoon she went over to the house and went into the kitchen. She was always very close to Nando. Sometimes he used to give her massages. She claimed that his massages were the only things that could help her get rid of her headaches.

"She called out but nobody was there. She waited outside until Nando's daughter, Beth, came home. She was eight. She went in the house and came out a few seconds later, screaming that a dog had eaten her father's face away.

"Millie went into the house. They were both dead in the hall. Nando was slumped in the chair with the shotgun in his lap. He had put the muzzle of the gun in his mouth and pulled the trigger with his toe. His whole face was shot away. His wife was on the floor. He had covered her up real nice with a sheet. He made five children orphans that day. His youngest daughter was only three.

"Millie broke down after she saw the body. She had to have shock treatments. She never has been the same since.

"I went into the house the next day. The place was such a terrible mess. Used Kotex in the hall. A bucket of slops that hadn't been emptied for days. She was just a terrible housekeeper.

"I've got to say that I always liked Hernando. He was very nice to me. When he came back from France, he brought me a silver fork that I still have somewhere."

Back in my room at the motel, Ina's words keep repeating in my head. *She wasn't a good housekeeper. She had a weak face. No chin. He brought me a fork from Germany. He covered her up real nice.*

Finally I get up and double-lock the door of my room. I am afraid of all the images that keep forming in my mind. I know I am locking the door to keep that story out of my life. But it just keeps slipping deeper and deeper into me. I say to myself: *I am Hernando. My father is Hernando. We are all Hernando. It is in our blood.* I can almost taste the mustard gas in my lungs and I want to cough.

In the morning I go down to the local newspaper office and thumb through the old papers. And there it is, on the front page:

LOCAL LABORER KILLS WIFE, THEN TAKES OWN LIFE

Bodies Discovered By Young Daughter

Using a double-barreled shotgun as a weapon, Hernando Andrews, 53, shot and killed his wife, Yvette Bailey Andrews, 33, and then ended his own life in their home on the North Road of this town. Medical examiner, Walter H. McIntyre of Augusta, said it was a case of murder and suicide. Death in each case was instantaneous.

Little is known of the actual circumstances of the tragedy that took the lives of the parents of five children.

The gruesome discovery of the bodies was made as four of the children alighted from the school bus at 3:15 P.M. Arriving at the Andrews home at the same time was Mr. Andrews's aunt, Mrs. Allen Parker of the Parkfield Road, who had called to inquire about the health of her nephew. Failing to find father or mother about the kitchen or living room, Beth Andrews, 8, opened the door from the living room into a hallway, to be greeted by the sight of her father lying on his back between the foot of the stairs and the front door of the house. Rushing into the hall, she screamed, "Daddy's in the hall with a gun in his lap."

The children conveyed the news to a neighbor and close friend of Mrs. Andrews, Miss Carmen Olson, who with her brother, Frank Olson, went to the Andrews house. There they found Mrs. Andrews lying on her back in the narrow hallway. Andrews had apparently pointed the gun at his face and released the trigger with his toe. His face was entirely shot away. They called Dr. A. C. Rich, who, responding quickly, found that husband and wife were dead. Dr. Rich notified Deputy Sheriff Walter Miller, who in turn called in the sheriff's office in Augusta and State Police officers Alphonse Whitman of Arbor and Frederick Knudsen of Clinton.

A neighbor told officers that she had talked to Mrs. Andrews about 2:00. How long after that hour the shooting took place has not been determined.

Sheriff Henry Pickwick made an examination of the case as the medical examiner gave permission for the removal of the bodies. Both bodies were taken to the Eldridge Funeral Home in Lakeland.

Other children who arrived at the home from school were Maxine, 12, Janet, 10, and Miriam, 3. A son, Ike, 17, was in Unity at the time with the Bailie High School baseball team.

Andrews was said by members of the family and neighbors to have been in ill health and a highly nervous condition for some time. He had been employed for two years by Lennon Brothers Carpenters as a carpenter. He had not been to work for two weeks, giving illness as a cause, his employers said.

Andrews was a veteran of World War I and was reported to have suffered from the effects of gas during his service in France. He enlisted at an early age in Company H, Second Marine Infantry, when that regiment was called for service at the Mexican border in 1916. He was with the regiment when it was ordered to France in 1917.

Their home is on the North Road about a mile south of the village and overlooking Lotus Pond.

Andrews was born in China on Nov. 2, 1899. He was the son of Albert and Florence Kincaid Andrews. He leaves two sisters, Mrs. Richard S. Mason and Mrs. Reena Bailey, Portland. Mrs. Andrews was a native of Pittsfield, the daughter of Jesse Bailey of Albion and Mrs. Mavis Bailey of Hartland. She had three brothers, Philip, Lemuel, and Kirk, and three sisters, Bethany, Beulah, and Gertrude.

The bodies are at the Eldridge Funeral Home, 10 Elm Street, Lakeland. Funeral arrangements will be announced.

When I check the date of the newspaper, I see that Hernando killed his wife just three days after Mother's Day.

I wonder if Deputy Sheriff Walter Miller is the son of Albert Miller, who sent Hernando's mother to the poor farm over fifty years before.

I remember spending Thanksgiving at my parents' before I came up here. I was talking to my father about how trivial and absurd life seems to have become in our time. In a voice like dry flaking skin, he replied that his life had always been meaningless. He would rather he had never been born.

"You are born alone and you die alone and no one really cares." Later on, he said that he had never trusted anyone he had ever worked with. "They will only stab you in the back if you give them a chance."

When he said that his life was meaningless, we all knew what he meant. We had all failed him. My brother and I had given his life no meaning. Nor had his wife. Not even his little grandson, who sat in a high chair, drunk with food, rolling his eyes.

A little later, I was talking to him about my stepson.

"I feel," I said, "as if I were really his father because I have been living with him as his father for so many years."

A frantic look came into my father's eyes. He began to tremble. In a voice choked with emotion, he said, "It doesn't matter one way or another. Sons never have any gratitude for what their fathers do for them. Sons never really love their fathers."

Hearing his words, I began to cry.

My mother screamed out at my father, "That's a terrible thing to say."

We were all silent. My father got up and left the room. After a few minutes, my brother and I followed him into the living room. We were sitting in silence when my mother came into the room with a steaming cup of coffee. Very deliberately, she walked up to my father and threw the coffee in his face.

"That was a terrible thing to say. You've always said the wrong things all your life. You are the cruelest man I have ever known."

He sat there for a few minutes with the coffee streaming down his face. Then, without a word, he got up and left the room and went upstairs.

When it was time for me to leave, my father walked me out to my car. A little boy was playing in the next yard. My father made a point of going over to him.

"I haven't seen you around for a long time."

The boy nodded and twirled himself around on the grass, so young and awkward and unformed that as he turned it almost seemed as if he had left some part of himself behind.

"It's very sharp," he said, brandishing his stick and throwing it into the grass. "It cuts grass."

My father walked back to me, smiling.

"That's some little fellow," he said, almost in wonderment.

I didn't see anything particularly exceptional about the child, however. What impressed me was my father's perfect contact with him. And his ravishing tenderness. And I wondered why I hadn't ever been "some little fellow" for him.

Today Ina told me the story about what happened to my father's sister Reena. She was adopted by a couple who dressed her like a little doll. When she was thirteen, she went to the police because the man was molesting her. But the judge made her go back to live with him again.

After she got old enough, she left them and got married. Her first child was a girl. When the girl was still a baby, Reena would sometimes feed her in the morning and then go off to work, leaving the child alone until late at night when she would come home from the saloon with a man.

When the child got into her teens, Reena sent her to the Home for Girls. The same place her mother had sent her years before.

It seems as if it never stops. We just go on passing it from one generation to another. My father never had a father. So he couldn't be a father. And now I find it so hard to be a father myself.

Yesterday afternoon, I had called my father and told him about Ina. I suggested that he call her. I didn't tell him anything about what else I had discovered about the family, nor did he ask.

He called today while I was there, just as I had hoped he would.

From what I could hear, they were both very stiff and formal with each other. He didn't ask any questions. She didn't volunteer any information.

▼

Even with the lights on in the middle of the day, the cellar was always dark. There was just a faint yellow glow that hung around the light bulbs.

Because it was so dark, I was always afraid that he would miss and hit me on the face. I never really knew whether he would be able to stop beating me once he had started. I had seen him destroy the kitchen at least twice, tearing apart cabinets with his bare hands, shattering all the glassware on the floor, shards of glass everywhere. Pots and pans flying everywhere. Pounding at the walls with his fists as if he were trying to smash the house to bits. Once he had even torn the door off its hinges.

Down in the basement, I had such a sense of my puniness. I wouldn't be able to see him. He would stand behind me in the darkness with his strap. He would seem so huge. And I was acutely aware of my spindliness, and of my nakedness that seemed to glow in the dark. Sometimes it seemed to me as if each blow from his lash would beat me right into the floor.

My imagination of his rage as I stood there shivering made him seem enormous. It felt almost as if I expected him to club me with the whole weight of the room. As if he had become the room with all its implicit weight and strength. His arm when it came down always seemed like a giant's hand.

"I didn't mean to do it."

"Get your hands away."

"Oh, Daddy, please. Don't. I promise to be good."

"I'm telling you for the last time. Get your hands away."

"Oh, Daddy. Please. No. Please stop. That's enough. I'll be good. I promise. I'll be good."

"I'm not going to start counting until you stop screaming."

"I'll be good. I'll be good. I promise. I promise."

"If you don't stand still, I'm really going to hurt you."

"Please, Daddy. Please."

68

His machines were stacked up all around me. Lathes, drill presses, cutting machines, kick presses, milling machines. The straps he used to beat me with were also used to run his machines. There were heaps of metal shavings and debris all over the floor. I always wondered if sometime he might not just pick me up and throw me against one of those machines. Or, even worse, cut me up in one of them. The shadows of those machines were particularly frightening. Sometimes I would go down in the cellar alone, just to stand beside them and quiver.

At some point my mother would always come down in answer to my screams. I would always know that she was standing right at the top of the stairs, only waiting for the right moment to intervene.

"Matt, stop it this instant. You'll hurt him."

"Get out of this, Martha. It's not your business."

"Matt. I just won't have you hurting him."

"You told me to punish him."

"I didn't tell you to kill him. You always go too far. Greggy, you go up to your room. You've been punished enough."

"Stay right where you are. We are going to settle this once and for all."

"Matt. He's been punished enough."

"Martha. You've got to stop interfering."

"You always go too far. I can't trust you to do anything."

"I'm not going to argue about it."

"Matt. I don't care. I'm not going to stand by and let you hurt this boy. Greggy. You just march upstairs to your room. Let me handle this. Just go now. You heard me."

"All right, Martha. He's your responsibility. I'm not going to do anything anymore. I'm just going to wash my hands of him."

And he never seemed to know what was happening, even though I did and I was only a child. When she would come downstairs, he would literally crumble. For an instant, his whole body would seem about to be torn apart by convulsions of internal rage. His eyes would pop and his muscles would tighten almost to the breaking point. When he spoke, it was almost like a moan. He was beating me for her sake. Because it made him feel like a good husband. Because she had asked him to beat me. Because I was bothering her. Because I was making life miserable for her. He was beating me because he wanted to earn her respect and gratitude. He was really just doing her bidding. But he was actually just a tool, and he never seemed to catch on.

Cut off. How could any man have been so cut off from everyone and still remain alive? Cut off from his wife. From his children. From other people. From himself. It is all the same thing. To never tell me a single story about his childhood. Never a single anecdote about his life. To never share his love for me. To never put his arms around me or hug me or kiss me. To never ask me a single question about my life or about the people I knew except as part of some angry inquisition into the facts of some infamy I was supposed to have committed. His absolute opacity. Nothing to break his silence except anger.

My father never touched me so far as I know except in anger or when I was asleep. I can't consciously remember his arms ever being around me. Except that sometimes when I fell asleep downstairs I would have a sense of being lifted up and carried up to my room as if by a god. I would awaken the next morning in my bed.

I was always embarrassed when he would talk to my friends. He would be so warm and friendly and almost paternal with them. It made me wonder even more what was wrong with me.

I remember the day when he drove me to school. A couple of boys said some very disparaging things about me in front of him. I was crushed. My father got furious. Not at them but at me. That night he raged at me. Blaming me for all the things they had said to me, as if I had arranged the scene deliberately as a personal insult to him.

I was the one who gave him mumps. He ate some spinach off my plate before I was completely cured. For two weeks afterward he lay in bed, sick and helpless. I didn't know it at the time, but he actually lost his left testicle because of the illness.

I was terrified of what would happen when he recovered.

He had an a priori conviction that I would somehow get in trouble with girls.

70

Once he beat me for not taking a girl home from a dance. Another time he beat me because I left a girl in a drugstore and went home without her.

Even when I wasn't to blame, I wasn't able to convince him. Once some kid at a party called up a girl and pretended to be me. I guess he talked very dirty to the girl. Tried to set up some kind of liaison in the woods. Her father called mine. I got beaten. Confined to my room for weeks.

I remember the time when I was thirteen and I tried to get some kid to take nude photos of his sister. Naturally, he got discovered. Her father called mine. I was in the room when the call came. My father put down the phone and told me to go upstairs and wait. I knew exactly what had happened.

It was late fall. As I waited, it got darker and darker. By the time I heard his footsteps ascending the stairs, it was almost pitch-dark.

He came into the room and turned on the light. He was trembling and ashen-faced. I watched him from the corner of my bed as I would have watched death approaching. He had beaten me so many times. It seemed as if killing were the only greater punishment left to him. He sat down in a chair across the room from me with a peculiar smile on his face like the flush of candlelight. It was the first time I could ever remember him sitting with me alone in my room. His presence was almost as awesome to me as the discovery of my crime.

"I suppose you know who that was on the phone?"

"Yes."

"Her father is very disturbed. I don't know what we are going to do with you yet. He is going to think it over."

Her father had also told him that I had been sending her letters threatening to rape her, and following her home from school. It was true that I had followed her home from school, but I didn't remember writing her any letters. But I had thought about raping her so many times and I couldn't really be sure.

"How do you know about such things?"

"What things?"

"The things you do with girls."

"Talking to people."

"What do you talk about?"

"Tell jokes. Things like that."

"Tell me some."

"I can't remember." Pushing myself back into the corner against the wall.

"You better remember because I am going to sit here until you do. This isn't going to be settled until I know everything."

So I began to tell him all the dirty jokes I could remember. When that didn't satisfy him, I made up a few more. I couldn't get the idea out of my head that he was trying to lay an insidious trap for me.

"Tell me what kind of things you do with girls when you go out with them."

"We hold hands. Sometimes I kiss them good night."

"What else?"

"Nothing."

"What else?"

"Sometimes I put my arm around them in the movies."

"What else?"

"Nothing."

"Do you want me to bring your mother up here? I'm not playing games with you. I want to keep her out of this, but if you force me to, I'll have to bring her into this right now."

"Sometimes I touch their breasts."

"What else?"

"Nothing else."

"How do you touch them?"

"What do you mean?"

"Do you pinch them? Do you hurt them?"

"No. I touch them very gently." So they wouldn't know what I was doing.

"You know that you have to be very careful when you touch a girl's breast. They are very sensitive. You can give them cancer."

His smile was like a bonfire.

It was just about a week after that discussion that my mother contrived to show me her nude body as if by accident. It was the first time I had ever seen the naked body of a woman.

⩋

Today I went to visit my Great-aunt Bessie, sister of Ina. Driving past the frozen lakes. The jackets of ice around the trees in the ponds, like the tutus of ballerinas.

Only address I had. *The house of Nora Summers.* Sounds to me like the dwelling of a witch.

My Aunt Bessie. Toothless. Hard of hearing. Incredibly gentle. Fine white fur on her face.

Cat on the stove.

I was never really sure whether she had any idea who I was. But we enjoyed each other.

In the afternoon I went to visit one of Reena's ex-husbands (she had four), who is in a nursing home. He is eighty-three years old. Utterly toothless and delightful. He didn't really want to talk to me, because he had fallen in love with one of the nurses and he was almost delirious with the possibility that she might be wheeling him upstairs at any minute.

He doesn't believe that any of the children he had with my aunt were even his own. They don't look at all like him.

"She always liked to keep a man or two on the side."

She was just a "poor thing." She had a "wild name." She was "kind of sly."

"I can't claim that any of the children were my own, because she was wild before each one of them. She needed two or three men all the time.

"She had kind of a floppy figure—200 to 245 pounds. She was always getting into trouble. Picking up loose ends, if you know what I mean."

I am beginning to lose heart. It is all I can do to stay. I find it hard even to think about writing in my journals at night. All I want to do is crawl into the oblivion of sleep.

I was always wearing his clothes. Putting on his tie clip. His ties.

Whenever I went out on dates, I would wear his camelhair coat, even though it was ludicrously too big for me. It gave me a special sense of power.

I would steal money from his pockets. I was always ashamed of doing it. I didn't understand what I was really doing. That it was just another way of putting on his clothes.

When I was thirteen, sitting in arithmetic class one day, I decided to change my name. Gregory hadn't done me very much good as a name, so I thought I would try my father's name, Matthew. Of course, everyone thought it was strange that I would change my name. It just made me seem even odder.

Machines were the passion of my father's life. His hunger for love and human contact was somehow reified into the realm of mechanical contrivances. His ultimate despair over human beings and human contact found a curious kind of apotheosis in the passion and intensity of his relationship to machines, in the conversion of inanimate substances into coherent forms of energy.

All the force of his life went into finding out how things work and how to make them work in new ways. His machines never deserted him. They always waited for him patiently in the cellar. He made love to his machines. They gave him all his succor and transcendence. They made no demands on his feelings. They asked for a totally selfless devotion.

That was precisely what my father had to give. A silent devotion without self or words. He found the consummation of his existence in the depth of his communion with machines.

I spent the day tramping in the woods with Cleavis, my father's first cousin, the son of Mildred, Ina's sister.

Hernando had taught him how to hunt. Cleavis didn't want to talk about Nando or hear anything about him that could in any way be considered critical. He loved Nando. He was determined not to have his memory contaminated by other people's experiences.

Almost everywhere we walked, Cleavis remembered shooting something. A ten-point deer here, a woodchuck there.

He pointed out the places where he'd been with Nando. The stream where Nando took thirty pelts with one trap. The stream where he caught spawning salmon with his bare hands.

Stories of dances. "Somebody would go looking to beat somebody up and somebody else would go looking to get beat up and they would both find what they wanted."

The way someone treats him is "the way he used me."

Cleavis's consideration. Bringing along candy bars for me.

The sun rippling through the trees as we pass. Gnarled oak trees like angry deformed prophets.

"Alder makes the nicest fire. There's good warmth in it."

A dead steer with still warm pleading eyes. A steer is a "critter." A dead steer has seen the "last of its living."

Cleavis's admiration for Nando, who knew all the signs and habits of animals. What they fed on. Where they went to find it. How to get the wind right. How he would think nothing of jogging four or five miles for partridge or a rabbit.

"He had the patience to wait. Couldn't nothing move him once he got settled down."

He was a "rank" man. A man who knew his own mind. There was no stopping him once he got started. He wouldn't back down. If he told a kid to do something, then that was the right thing to do.

The thing about Nando was that he always had time for boys.

River picking up color from the sky and reflecting it back on the clouds. White birch like sentinels.

Marks of a "just traveling deer." A deer that didn't actually live in the neighborhood.

Visit to the old farmhouse on the "Maxwell road," where my father was born. Family graveyard hidden in the snow. Two massive oaks over 150 years old. Four Civil War graves.

Talking about the old farm. "Nothing like the sight of beans in bloom."

Afterward I visited Aunt Mildred, Ina's sister, and her husband, Allen. Mildred wouldn't see me until she had had a chance to go to the hairdresser's and have her hair done. Her long silver tresses are her crowning glory.

Her supper was a round mound of mashed potatoes that covered her entire dinner plate.

Her husband, Allen, is her pride and joy.

Mildred was very close to Nando. When she got lice, Nando would wash her hair and comb it out with a fine-toothed comb after dousing her head with rubbing alcohol. He also massaged Millie's legs after they had been frozen once and there was the possibility of gangrene.

A few days before the murder, Millie gave Nando some of her nerve medicine.

She remembers Nando twirling a glass once and saying, "I'm going and I'm going to take her with me."

Millie added that "He really liked her. He didn't kill her out of malice."

Allen told me about my grandfather's ingenuity. Once he fashioned a jig saw out of a sewing machine. Another time he built himself a bull cart. He also made himself the first house on wheels in this part of the country. Used to haul it around from place to place.

When I heard this, I could feel my whole face light up. This is the first positive thing I have heard about my grandfather.

A few days ago, Ina caught my eye and told me, almost as if she were repeating an article of faith, "My father never shouted or slapped anyone."

Yesterday, it was a different story. Her father would go into town and sell butter and eggs for whiskey. He would come home thick in the tongue and pick fights.

Once he grabbed a frying pan off the stove and threatened to hit his wife. Ina had to intervene.

Today Ina told me her father had another woman he used to go stay with in Vermont for months at a time. He would come back to his wife, Ida, when he was near death from drink and debauchery. Ida would nurse him back to health without a word of reproach. When he was well, he would go back to the other woman.

Ina could never remember any sign of affection or tenderness passing back and forth between her mother and father.

Ina's eyes, as she tells me this, are utterly remorseless. I wonder if her father ever saw that look in her eyes.

"My mother was a saint. She never said a word to my father when he was alive. After he died, she only blamed herself. She used to say, 'If only I could have done more for him.' "

Just as I was leaving, she got a certain look in her eye.

"There is something I shouldn't tell you."

"You can tell me anything."

"You promise never to tell anyone."

"Yes."

"Your grandfather used to beat his dogs. Once I saw him whipping his bulldog with a chain and hitting him in the ribs."

Afterward, I spent the afternoon with Jake Whalen, a man who knew my grandmother most of her life. He quoted Florence as saying, "No one can ever say I ran around with men. I married them."

"She must have had a hot box somewhere. She knew how to play the snappers." Meaning, I guess, that she knew how to attract men with her sexuality.

Then he told me that my grandmother had once told him that her father had raped her when she was a child. He had raped all his daughters when they reached a certain age. It was common knowledge around these parts.

Ina had known I was going to see him. Almost the minute I got back to the motel, she was on the phone. With a sobbing voice, she explained that not a word of it was true.

"It never happened that way. If it had, I wouldn't be the kind of woman I am."

I repeated exactly what the man had told me. She replied,

"Well, maybe he did it to Florence or to the neighbors' children, but he never did it to me."

I know Ina is telling me the truth. She could never be the person she is if that had happened to her. But Florence.

Somehow it seems to explain everything. At least it is a reason. At this point any reason is better than none.

I spent the morning with Ike, Hernando's oldest son. He was glad to see me.

Ike described Nando as "a hard man who believed that people should do things right." There was hardly a day of his life that Nando didn't beat him, as well as his second oldest sister, Janet.

Ike had had an idea of what was going to happen. On the day of the murder, he had actually considered taking the firing pin out of his father's rifle. His father had begged him to stay home with him. But Ike was supposed to play in a ball game.

After it happened, they came and got him.

He is still living with the woman he was going to run away with to Boston almost twenty years ago, when he was still a boy. Her brother, the man his mother was going to run away with, is also living with them.

She took photos of us standing together. My arm around his shoulder. When I touched this cousin whom I had never seen before, I got gooseflesh all over my skin.

In the afternoon I drove down to the Togus Veterans' Hospital, where Ike's father, my Uncle Hernando, tried to sign himself in.

Two rows of stately fir trees line the entrance. Smell of pine needles in the air. White snow. Silver clouds with the silver-yellow sun shimmering through in places.

A stage setting for eternity.

Sign: "DRIVE CAREFULLY. PROTECT OUR PATIENTS."

Two churches. Pray for the dead and the dying.

Inside the hospital, the patients have a ghostly silver-yellow aura just like the winter sky, as they sit in their dirty coarse white hospital gowns. Rivulets of age like dirt running down their faces.

I have decided to leave Arbor. There is nothing else I want to know.

In the evening I said goodbye to Ina with such mixed feelings. It was hard to tear myself away. And yet I could hardly bring myself to stay with her as long as I did. I know I will be seeing her again. I promised I would bring my father with me the next time I come.

Tomorrow I am driving down to Northwood, New Hampshire, to see what I can find out about Al Andrews's parents.

I am trying hard to convince myself that I am glad to have made this trip. I'm sure someday I will be. Right now my whole sense of my life has been fractured. I am terrified of suddenly discovering all my newfound relatives inside myself.

I know they are all there. I know they've always been there inside my genes. But when I think about them, my head starts to pound.

Yet in one sense I am glad they are so awful. Somehow it redeems me. I know that I am not alone in the pain of my struggle to live. It is not just that I have found that I am part of my family history. In some strange way it is as if I have become all men.

I am not alone anymore. I am everyone. Al and Florence, Nando (particularly Hernando), Andrew, Ida, Ike, Reena, Ina, Millie, Cleavis and all the rest. And all the names I don't know and never will know.

Now I know how vast and inexplicable and trackless my own life is. Having my past frees me from all standards of judgment. I don't have to have my false pride anymore. They were the way they had to be. And I am the way I have to be and it is the same for all men and women in their endless searching. If only I can hang on to this sense of life.

As I drive out of Arbor, the countryside is iridescent. Snow-capped, picturesque old farmhouses. Glistening, ice-covered ponds. Michelangelo sky. Stands of pine trees. Sudden ravines. Robin's-egg-blue sky.

All I can think of is: *I am getting away. I am not going to die in Arbor.* I feel the sense of the past closing in on me. Implicating me. I say to myself: *I am getting away. I don't belong to the past.*

I can feel my face glowing. And I say: *I belong to the living. I belong to myself and not to my dead and dying ancestors.*

First I am going to New Hampshire to track down Al Andrews's family. Then I'm going to visit my mother's sister in Portland, Maine. Then I'm going home. But where is home for me?

New Hampshire

I drive all the way to Northwood through a squalling snowstorm. I arrive at the clerk's house just before dark. The town is too small to have a courthouse. The snow is almost up to my ankles.

All the records are kept in a musty back room. The clerk has no time, so I have to find my own way through the records. For a long time there isn't anything. Then everything comes together.

On his marriage certificate, my grandfather had listed his mother's maiden name as Mary E. Goodwin. I went over the names again and again, but I couldn't find anyone by that name who had married an Andrews.

Then I notice a marriage between Mary E. Goodwin and John Rofs. I remember that "f" was a way of writing "s" back in those days. This made her Mary Ross. I remember seeing earlier that John B. Andrews, a farmer who was thirty-six years old, had married a Nellie Ross, a widow who was thirty-three years old. Nellie, I guess, is short for Elizabeth, Mary E.'s middle name.

Checking further, I find that a live male was born to John B. Andrews and Nellie M. Andrews on November 5, 1878. That date is the same as John Albert Andrews's birth date. So I have found my great-grandparents.

My great-grandfather, John B. Andrews, died on March 31, 1878, of consumption, seven months before his son's birth.

In a privately printed book that the clerk has on the history of Northwood, I find a note indicating that, early in the 1880's, the Andrews farm was sold to a John Milton and his mother. Why?

John Andrews had many relatives who could have helped his widow. Did they turn against her for some reason? Did it have something to do with Al and the circumstances of his birth? Did his relatives believe that he wasn't really John Andrews's son?

Then I find this passage in the book:

> Bands of gypsies traveled the roads of New Hampshire through Northwood, stealing stray hens and everything else they could lay their hands on, including clothes from the clothesline. At the cry, "The gypsies are coming," all the livestock was put in the barns, clothes gathered from lines, tools and toys put away. Reluctant children were stashed in houses. Doors and windows were bolted.
>
> In the gypsy camp there were fires with bubbling cauldrons, dark-eyed brightly dressed women, fighting cocks, music of fiddles, and the sound of gypsy laughter.

In the one photo I have of Al, he looks so much like a gypsy. Dark curly hair. Swarthy skin. Mischievous gypsy eyes.

Could my great-grandfather's relatives have turned against Nellie Andrews because they suspected Al was the son of a gypsy?

Al Andrews, who built himself a house on wheels and dragged it from place to place. Who could never keep a job. Who was so clever with his hands. Who could make a jig saw out of a sewing machine.

Could it be? Of course. It couldn't have been any other way.

Afterward, I go to visit the author of the book. She possesses the diary of my great-great-uncle, Samuel Andrews, John B. Andrews's brother. She won't let it out of her hands.

I have time to copy out only two entries before I have to leave:

> Pleasant cut out some light broad clothes and Mark Hart cut me a pair of pantaloons. Carried them up to Jonathan's to be made. Then went to Bartlett's tavern. While I was there, Charles Foster came and said that mother had hung herself. Shocked, I immediately started with horse and sleigh that he came out in, and Uncle Jonathan with me arrived at home and went in. They had brought Mother down from the garret where she hung herself and laid her on the floor. This was the most distressing sight that I ever saw. I gazed upon her pale counte-

nance and with a heart almost bursting with sorrow I withdrew to give vent to my overflowing feelings. To increase if possible the intensity of my feelings, there I beheld my Father and my brother and sister overwhelmed with grief. Several of the neighbors were in, however. This night, Jefferson and Loverly set up as watches. She was deranged.

The day she committed suicide, she appeared robust in the morning, as well as she had for some time, No one was at home, except Dolly and Daniel, I having gone to the road and my father and John were in the woods and Aunt who had never been away before were gone to Mrs. Foster. Dolly said that Mother went up to the garret to bring down the clothes today. Brought down one armful and as she thought went back to get another. She however did not come down and my sister thought she might be making the beds. She did not come down and my sister went up chamber to see where she was. Not finding her there, my sister was afraid to go up garret so she went and called Daniel. He went up and found her hanging, a cord around her neck. He immediately cut the cord and let her down but her breath had fled then. He called in the neighbors. They endeavored to bring her to, but she was too far gone. Text 45 Psalm, 1 verse. Everything conducted with decency and order. Chimney caught fire about 2 o'clock.

I want to go back home so badly now. I am almost desperate to leave. I don't care what I find anymore. I'm just going through the paces. There is so much more I could do in Northwood.

Visit the old house. Find old relatives. I know there must be just as much of a story here as there was in Maine.

But I don't want it. I can admit that now. I can't stand anymore. My patience and tolerance are at an end. I have come to the end of rope. My own rope. I've lost even the will to write about what I am finding out. I live by rote now.

I'm going to visit my mother's sister and that is the end.

I spend the day in Portland with my mother's sister. My Aunt Irma, who never got over the stigma of being the plain sister with the crippled leg. And yet who is still a sexy woman in her own way, even though she is over sixty-five.

"Mama was a beautiful woman. She liked the men and the men liked her."

My aunt is clearly excited by the memory of her mother's sexiness. My spinsterish aunt who didn't marry until she was over forty.

"Papa was away a lot in the merchant marine, and Mama would go out to the bars and pick up men and bring them home. She loved her liquor."

For some reason, my aunt takes a malicious delight in revealing all these details about my grandmother.

"And the men always followed Mama around because she was so beautiful. After Papa died, Mama used to take our older sister, Virginia, out with her to the bars. Virginia was very beautiful too. And they would bring home men together.

"After Mama died, your mother went to live with Aunt Belle and Uncle John. After John drank carbolic acid, there was a lot of talk about sending your mother to an orphanage. But Cousin Martha arranged for her to stay with Papa's brother, Uncle Edwin, instead. Uncle Edwin, who met his wife, Cerity, in a brothel in New Orleans."

As she tells me this particularly juicy bit, my aunt's eyes sparkle.

If I go on with Irma much longer, I won't have any illusions left.

"Did you know that Ronald, your father's twin brother, was a homosexual?" She wags her head salaciously. "Oh, yes, he was. It was no secret. Once he went to New York with two other boys and they cleaned him out. Took all his stuff."

Oh, yes, I knew. It is one of those things I admit to myself only very rarely. I remark that we are a strange family.

"You bet we are. And one of the strangest is your mother. Do you know that all during the time your father was working down in Florida and your mother was alone in Connecticut, she stayed upstairs in her room with the door locked and a butcher knife by her side, except when she went out to the store?"

But she really doesn't have to tell me that. I know that in one way or another my mother has always spent her life locked up in a room, armed against the whole world.

86

The snow is getting very deep in Maine and I am getting very tired. I think I am through with the past for a while. I am going home.

But there is still one more thing I have to do. On my way back, I stop off in Boston to visit the Little Wanderers Orphanage, where my father and Ronald and Nando were sent almost seventy years ago.

Everything has changed. It is no longer an orphanage, but a treatment center for disturbed children. The caretaker will let me see only the dining room because the children are upstairs sleeping. It is still as it was over seventy-five years ago. In the main wall, there is an enormous stained-glass window depicting a mother and a small boy with a dog standing by her side.

Always there. Still there for all the little wanderers every time they sit down to eat, to remind them of all they have lost.

New York

My father is very insistent to learn about everything I found out. He wants to know particularly why his mother got married so many times and why she gave up her children. He won't accept any evasions.

"Well, what did you find out?" Apprehensive and suspicious. Chin lowered defensively.

"Her father is supposed to have molested her."

"What does that mean?"

"He physically abused her."

He is getting angry. He won't accept any more euphemisms.

"What are you saying?"

"Well, she told someone that he raped her when she was a child. That would explain a lot of things."

He looks away and becomes very quiet. After a while, he gets up and crosses the room to a table and searches through a drawer. As he passes, I hear something like a sigh, a short blue sound of air heaved out.

My mother, who is never one to let things like that pass, hears it too.

"Your father sighs a lot these days. I'm always hearing him." Implicitly warning me not to meddle in her own past. And she mimics his sighs. Looking very proud of herself because she can reproduce them so accurately.

Later, in the kitchen, I ask her about something else her sister Irma told me.

"Why didn't you ever tell me that you had lived in Brooklyn

when you were growing up? Maybe I'll go over and take a look at the house."

"Oh, no. Don't do that, Greggy. Please." Pleading gently. "Don't start that up all over again." Frightened, almost hysterical, as the greater implications of what I might do begin to sink in. A sudden rush of tears.

"Haven't you done enough already? There are some things it is simply better to forget. If you think about the past too much, it can drive you crazy. I don't want you stirring up all that old stuff. It's over and done with. It doesn't do any good. I won't let myself become obsessed with the past. If I did, I wouldn't be able to go on living. It's not incest or anything like that." Guessing that I might think that was the cause of her fear.

But I am relentless.

"You can't hide from the past, Mother."

"I'm not hiding. It's just that I don't want to go into all that again."

"It was always your way to keep things hidden. I'm not saying you were wrong. Just that it has been your way."

"Well, your father is very disturbed. I think he is very upset. Finding out all those things about himself made him feel worthless."

Hearing those words, I feel hollow inside.

"It's true," she goes on. "I always kept things from him that he didn't need to hear, because he had such a temper."

Now I am lost. I don't know what my father's temper has to do with her fear of the past. Yet I know that somehow my mother has finessed me completely, and that I will never get back to her.

"He was always so violent. I always knew just what I had to do to handle him."

That was the myth that my mother and father shared. That he would go berserk without my mother to control him. That myth was his cage. But it was her cage too, because she spent her whole life locked up inside it with him.

I realize she is telling me how angry she is with me for meddling where I didn't belong. Warning me not to go any further. So there is nothing more to be said. I drop Brooklyn and go back to my father in the other room.

Later, I ask him how he feels about what I have found out.

"I think I would have rather not known. All except for Ina. She makes it sort of worthwhile."

Yet, a few minutes later, he talks about wanting to buy the old family place in Maine. And when I suggest that I walk to the railroad station to catch my train back to the city because it is such a pleasant day, he insists that he drive me because it will give us more time to spend together.

This morning the phone rang. I picked it up. There was my mother, sobbing and hysterical. Most of her words were swallowed up by her tears.

She doesn't want me to go on. I have to call a stop to my investigations now.

"You can't make me do it, Greggy. No one can. I can't rack up all those old memories again. I just can't do it. If I do, I'll just go insane. It was hard to live through all of that stuff once, without having you rack it up all over again. You will just have to understand."

My mother's silence. It always seemed as if my mother told me everything. Now I realize that she didn't tell me anything at all about what really mattered to her. Nothing about her mother or her father or her older sister. The deepest memories. The real truth was just as unbearable to her as my father's had been to him.

She talked so much and told so many stories that I always imagined she told me everything. Now I realize that her life is really even more of a mystery than my father's.

A letter from Ina came today. Allen, my Great-aunt Mildred's husband, is dead at eighty-one.

Ina writes: "You are one of the family now."

I am forty-three years old and yesterday I touched my father's skin for the first time. I have shaken his hand. Brushed against him.

But I have never really allowed myself to feel him.

He has always talked about his dry skin. And my mother has never stopped reminding him of it.

"I've always told him that anybody could find him if they wanted to. Like Hansel and Gretel with the bread crumbs. You'd just have to follow the trail of bits of desiccated skin that he leaves behind him everywhere he goes. I've never known anyone else in my whole life to have skin like that."

My father asked me if any of his relatives in Maine had skin like his. From a distance it looks like old, faintly yellowing parchment. Closer up, it is almost like a quilt, made up of a series of translucent parallelograms of skin joined together by faint ridges, like the skin of ice on a pond. Even though it is dry, it is so thin and soft to the touch that it is almost as if he had no skin at all. Because he is old now and has lost so much of his weight, his skin hangs in folds like the skin of a deflated balloon.

As I was touching my father's skin, my mother reminded us of the proper medical name for his condition. He has ichthyosaurian skin, lizard's skin.

I really couldn't answer his question about his relatives, because I hadn't even bothered to notice. Except it is true that Ina has skin very much like his. But she is eighty-one and her skin is probably just that way because of aging.

How afraid I was to talk to my father even four months ago. I used to go out and see my mother on days when I knew he would be away. That is, when he still left the house.

And when he was there, I could hardly wait for him to go upstairs for a nap, so I could talk alone with my mother. But my father wants me now.

He is the one who has asked if I can come out on days when he is here. He didn't even take his nap today.

I think we have entered into a courtship together. Very shy and tentative. We are giving each other a chance. Seeing how far we can go together.

He is really such an extraordinary man. He thinks. He is aware of so much more than I had ever imagined. His range of experience is so much broader than I ever knew. All that time, when I thought he was withdrawn and frozen in his rage, he was alive and thinking and feeling. His eye was always clear. He knew so much about the world, with his shy tender cynicism. He had his own values and his own sense of life. He never stopped trying to live with grace, and he never stopped trusting.

Today my mother tells me the story of how my father was once fired from a job, my father sitting right beside us in the room.

"He came home one Friday afternoon, pale as a ghost. Eyes shrunken. Turned around in his head. He couldn't eat. He went upstairs without any supper. Stomach was bothering him. Next day he couldn't eat breakfast. Finally he broke down sobbing. Moaning. Retching. Heaving."

Then my mother mimicked for us both the way in which he had said those words which must have been so terrible to him:

" 'I lost my job.'

"I asked him to tell me about it," she went on, continuing to mimic him.

" 'Got angry. They were trying to get me to do something I didn't think was right and I lost my temper.'

" 'Doesn't sound so bad. Go back on Monday and apologize.' " Mimicking her reply of so long ago and then turning to me.

"I went out and bought him a couple of model airplanes and sat him down at a card table. He spent all weekend working on the planes."

For the first time my father broke his silence. "You were really calm."

"On Monday," my mother continued her narration, "he went in to see his boss and apologized. They wouldn't give him back the same job he had but they allowed him to stay on in a lesser position."

For a long time the three of us sat in silence, looking at the floor. Were we all thinking the same thing? Remembering that the reason he had to go back to work immediately was that I was at Harvard and needed the money he was earning to meet my tuition payments?

Later on, when we were alone for a few minutes, I started talking very gently to my father about how much I had missed a relationship with him when I was growing up.

He started telling me about all the things he had done for me. Buying me clothes. Giving me money. Putting me through college. All the things my mother had always said she had forced him to do for me.

I told him that I hadn't wanted any of these things. What I wanted was his love. But he kept on reeling off his list of gifts, just the way my mother would have done. For an instant it was as if my mother herself were talking, instead of my father. The same words. The same tone that I had heard in her voice so many times.

With an air of disbelief, I told my father that he sounded just like my mother.

"Why not?" he answered. "She's a wonderful woman."

Later, thinking over this conversation, I became ridiculously happy. This was the first time that my father had ever given me any hint that he had actually wanted me to have all these things. That he hadn't really begrudged me. The family myth had always been that my mother had wrested all these things away from him against his will for my benefit, and that my father would get very angry if he ever found out what she had given me. So I had always lived a double life with him.

Now I see that they were his gifts too. My father had been giving to me all along. How fantastic!

I love to touch my father now. Today, I put my arms around his shoulders and rubbed his back. My fingers were so surprised by the almost total absence of flesh and muscle.

He is almost weightless now. After all these years, his flesh has worn away. It is hard for him to sleep because his bones are so cutting-sharp, honed by the erosion of time. They jab through his skin like knives whenever he puts any weight on them. He moves ethereally now, as if gravity had lost all its pull.

He sits in a chair like a fallen leaf. Mostly he likes to sit and watch the birds feeding in the back yard. And he is almost a bird himself. A sparrow or a wren. Nowadays all he eats is crumbs.

He told me about his boyhood in the forests in back of the Armstrong mansion at 69 Hammond Street. The fields of oak and elm. The tangled mazes of blueberries and strawberries and wild blackberries on which carpets of birds would come to feed. Sometimes huge stones bigger than houses would suddenly appear almost miraculously in the fields. There would be meadows with small trees and foliage and pits of stagnant water on top of them. These huge boulders were made up of millions of tiny water-polished stones held together by a resinous substance.

My father had a little terrier who used to chase weasels. It would stick its snout into their holes again and again, despite the damage to its nose. As he and his brother walked through the woods, red fox would scoot across their path. There were bobcats and rumors of bear. And deer tracks.

My father and his brother would play Indians. Sometimes they would shoot at each other with arrows. Once my father shot an arrow through his brother's leg.

We have never talked so carefully before. For so many years the only music we made was snarling. Now we try hard to find points of agreement and harmony. And we try to make those points of harmony last. It is almost as if we were making music when we talk together, trying to keep the harmony going, building it higher and higher.

There were never any men in that house, except protégés of his foster mother. "Little Mother's" only outlet was music, and she collected musicians, taking them into her house and becoming their benefactress.

The violinist who wore white gloves. The pianist who never shook hands. All those soft-handed men who could never bring themselves to touch my father.

My father went to public high school for one year. While he was there, he got a crush on the only male teacher in the school. He taught my father about automobiles and how they worked and how to drive them. They would go out driving together in the afternoon. For a while they were very close. Then my father left school and never went back. Is this why my father has always loved machines?

Searching for a man. Searching for a father.

My father went on to tell me that he didn't know the facts of life until he was twenty-four, when he married my mother. He said it didn't bother him. That none of it bothered him because he had no idea how other people lived or how people were supposed to live. He didn't have any idea what he was missing.

But somehow you know. He had friends outside the house. Boys talk. They read books about how other people live. Somehow they find out that other people care about their children and about each other. About mothers and fathers and what they are to each other. And sex. There is no way a boy can stop himself from learning about sex. It just bursts out of his body like a tree.

I suspect that in his anger against his real parents my father just blotted out all knowledge of the life process. He simply refused to hear. He simply refused to learn how babies were born.

And I wonder if that didn't have something to do with the fact that my father and his brother stopped going to high school when they were thirteen. Were they beginning to learn about that other life? Could they not bear to know how different they were? How different they would always have to be if they were going to survive?

In all the years he was with Mrs. Armstrong, there was the explicit understanding that if he didn't behave himself, he would have to go back to the orphanage. The years mounted up and yet his foster mother never once kissed him. Never once was he allowed into her bedroom. The limit of her loving was a pat on the back of the head.

In the eighteen years he lived with her, he never brought a friend home with him. When I told him that I thought his foster mother was irresponsible and that she should have made more of a commitment to him, he demurred very softly. She couldn't do any differently. It was just the kind of woman she was. The person whose fault it was was the doctor who brought the twins there from the orphanage. He should have known it was no place to raise children.

Yesterday my father went to the doctor's. As I was leaving today, he told me, "For the first time in my life, I was able to tell a doctor what my parents died of."

I couldn't stop smiling all the way home.

So much comes out unconsciously. My father was talking today about his twin brother, Ronald, and how everything had been given to Ronald while he had had to work for everything he got.

At one point my father couldn't remember his brother's name. My name came out first. Then my brother's. Finally on the third try, he found his brother's name.

My father always got second best from us too. The leavings after my mother had bestowed all her love on her sons. He was just telling me that it had been the same with his brother, who was also the favored one. And so he calls his brother by my name.

It is part of the same terrifying pattern of repetition that has been imposed on his life. That primal pattern—somewhere in his mind not only has my mother been his foster mother but I have been his brother.

And on the way home I found myself thinking about how inevitable it is that we repeat our lives and the lives of our parents over and over again.

My mother locked into her myth of Rob. Still regarding him as the threatening stranger after all these years.

My father endlessly recreating his life with his foster mother. My mother threatens him in the same way. Both of them denying him a permanent place in their lives. "If you ever hit me, I'll leave you." "If you don't behave, I'll send you back to the orphanage."

How does it happen? How do we do it to ourselves?

It is terrifying how we create the world and all its people so completely out of our expectations. Out of our need to repeat.

My mother still the orphan child. My father still the homeless boy.

We all seem to imprison each other in our dreams. In the vise of our past lives and past selves.

How do we ever get out? Wives and husbands repeating their past lives with each other. Parents and children. Reena and her daughter. Nando and his children (he made five children orphans that day; he was one of five orphans himself). Al, the man without a father who could never be a father. Florence raped by her father, throwing out all her children.

I also am my mother and father and I repeat their lives in mine. They are so much a part of me I don't even know where they begin or end in my life.

Recently my father's doctor told him that he had to start walking more. This reminded my mother of a story.

She got very animated the way she always does when she tells a story. Lips puckering as if she were sucking on a piece of candy. Her eyes roving mischievously. Body quivering in her chair like a cat about to pounce.

"You know how it was back in the Depression when we didn't have any money. Well, I've always loved cherries. When I was a little girl, if someone gave me five cents, instead of spending it on candy the way most kids would, I went out and bought a bag of cherries. Just ten or twelve little cherries.

"Well, on this particular day, Matt bought me a five-cent bag of cherries. Just ten or twelve little cherries. It was all the money he had, so he had to walk all the way from Forty-second Street to the Battery to catch his ferry. And you know how your father always hated to walk.

"When he gave me the cherries and told me what he had done, I told him what a stupid thing it was for him to have done. How stupid can you get, walking all that way just for a bag of cherries?"

All the while she was telling this story, she was smiling as if she were revealing a devastating secret. Her eyes had a kind of devious light around them as if they had picked up the aura of a flickering candle.

It is so easy to misunderstand her. To accept her declarations of disdain for him as representing her true feeling. It is a mistake I make all the time. On the face of it she is ridiculing my father. But underneath I think she is really talking about her sense that she really isn't worth anything. That anyone who would go to such trouble for her must be out of his mind. She can't acknowledge the depth of my father's feeling for her, so she has to mock it. Probably there is nothing more frightening to her than accepting the reality of his love. Could my mother have ever accepted him as he was? Could she have ever allowed herself to see him as he was? I suppose not, because she needed her dream of him too much. She could never have accepted that she had married someone so much like herself. A lonely, disillusioned orphan just like herself. To have admitted that would have only crushed all her hopes for transcending herself. His reality, so she seemed to believe, would have only made her reality unbearable. So she has to love and be loved through this peculiar camouflage of disdain.

But in the deepest part of herself she adores his love and cherishes it. That is probably the most closely held secret of her life.

I wonder if my father knows about her secret love for him. About the depths of her secret gratitude. I suppose he must. After all, they have lived with each other almost fifty years.

I'd like to think that if my mother had been more responsive, there might have been no limit to my father's giving.

But now I realize that isn't really true. Because nothing that had ever happened to him even remotely suggested that a woman could be generous to a man. He had no expectations. There was no place inside him to receive. No bed had ever been laid inside himself to receive a woman's love. Not by his mother, or by either of his two foster mothers. So he takes just as much from my mother as he could possibly accept from any woman. Just as she takes from him as much as she could take from any man.

Today, my father and I drove the used Jaguar I just bought down to the seashore to a garage owned by a friend of his. My father was very worried about me driving the car because it is so old and in such perilous condition. He doesn't know anything about Jaguars, so he didn't feel competent to look at it himself.

It was like so many of the Saturday mornings we used to spend together. Standing around and waiting in hardware stores or garages or shops. My father shy and diffident with everyone. Timeless. Lost in chattering. So patient. Never asserting himself. Always the last to be waited on.

I would stand off in one corner, frozen with rage because my father was only pretending to be with me. I was like a dog on a leash that was simply expected to wait for him.

It was the same on this day too. It was hours before the mechanic could get around to checking out the car.

It was warm and sunny when we started out. On the way back, it turned cold and clammy. We were only about ten miles from the garage on our way home when the car stopped dead. I couldn't get it started again. We got out and I opened up the hood. My father started examining the car, fiddling with this and that. Since his heart attack, he has gotten thin. His coat is about three sizes too big for him. I am so used to him as he was that, each time I look at him now, he seems to be shrinking right in front of my eyes.

His hands started to shake with cold and fear. He has always gotten upset when things don't work and when he can't repair them. All his life he has taken on himself the responsibility for making things work. As we continued to stand there in the cold wind, his whole body began to shake and his lips turned ashen. I suddenly realized that he was probably about to have another heart attack if he didn't stop what he was doing right away.

I practically had to tear his quivering fingers away from the ice-cold motor. I pushed my body in front of his. I started to examine the car myself, doing all the things that I remembered had to be done. My father still wouldn't get in the car, but he seemed relieved that I had taken over. He still stood there beside me, shaking like a leaf. I had to give up. I called for a tow truck and the two of us sat in the car and waited together.

I was concerned about him and I intervened. I told him what to do. I've never done that before. I have always deferred to him. It was the first time in my whole life I have ever told him what to do. And I knew he was grateful because he knew that he couldn't have managed to break himself away. And I think that he was almost sure that he was going to have a heart attack and die.

I could feel him depending on me. Leaning on me. Needing me to be there with him.

The car has brought us very close together. It is practically all we talk about now. And I know that for him, in some curious way, the car has become me. When he lifts the hood, it is clear that I have become the car for him and that all his feelings about me have been deflected onto the car. He is too shy and complicated to love me directly. He needs some object. And he has chosen the car. To him it is not inanimate metal. He feels about it the way other people would feel about a flesh-and-blood human being. His feelings come out on it and transform it.

Thinking back, I can see that it has always been this way. My father has always loved me or tried to love me through inanimate objects. My new car is not the only car which has figured in our emotional life. He has always loved my cars. Driven them as often as he could. Tried to keep them as long as he could. I never understood. I thought he was simply jealous of me and wanted to get my cars away from me so he could have them for himself.

But it wasn't like that at all. Having my car nearby made him feel close to me.

Everyone has such odd corners. Each life has so many beginnings. So many times, I forget that my father, the engineer, went to art school. That he knows all about etching and lithography. There are still casts of his sculpture down in the basement.

He claims that he had nothing original to say, no ideas of his own. I don't believe it. If he could have only trusted himself more.

I found out today that it was actually my mother who proposed marriage. Not a nameless someone as I had always been told. Not just a miraculous consensus among the four of them. Not my father as I had been led to believe. But my mother. "Why don't we all get married?" Her words out of her own mouth.

My mother was describing the event as she had so many other

103

times before. "And someone suggested we all get married."

And I saw a sudden look of perplexity on my father's face. He had heard this statement so many times before and never questioned it. But on this particular day, something unusual must have happened. Somehow his mind cut back through all those years of obfuscation and misrepresentation to a pure memory of the event.

"But it was you, Martha," he said with astonishment in his voice. As if he could hardly believe what he was saying himself. "You were the one who suggested it." As if he suddenly realized what a difference this simple fact made in his sense of the history of their lives together.

He wasn't the one. He hadn't forced her into marriage as he had gone on half-believing all these years. Now he remembered. My mother had actually proposed to him. For an instant it was as if the very house shook. When my mother heard his words and suddenly understood all that they implied, a sudden tremor went through her body. She turned her head toward him with a look of dismay. Wanting to deny what he had said because it contradicted one of the most basic myths of their lives together. And yet unable to deny it because she knew it was the truth. Hearing my father's words and seeing the expression on her face, I finally understood why she hadn't wanted to leave him when Cousin Martha tried to persuade her. It was because she had proposed. "I didn't want to make a fool out of him."

But my father knew. He knew all the time, but in his love for her he had managed to forget.

And instantly my mother's mind fled from this completely indigestible reminder of the truth back to her dream.

"And you had a hundred-dollar bill, didn't you, Matt? You always carried one."

But it was too late.

Standing there, I could almost read my father's thoughts. *So I didn't trick her into marriage after all. It was her idea. It really was. Somehow I had forgotten. Gotten it wrong. She was the one. I hadn't robbed the cradle. Stolen her youth away. She was the one.*

But these thoughts must have left his mind almost as quickly as they had entered. Because the myth contained a deeper truth than the facts. Without the myth he would have had to question too many things about his own life. Too many conceptions about himself would have to be re-examined. Nothing in his life could ever have prepared him to accept the beauty and innocence of his love for my mother.

This weekend I finally went up to Maine with my father as I had promised myself I would do before I went to California.

I met him at the train station in the city. We were both trembling. All our contradictory feelings for each other shook our bodies. I was so apprehensive that I even took him to the wrong airport and we missed our plane to Augusta. We had to fly to Boston instead and drive up in a rented car.

We spent the first morning with Ina, tramping around graveyards.

She has begun to treat them as if they were her home. Tidying up the plots and showing off the different graves as if they were rooms.

Afterward, we went to the old farm. The fields were covered with marsh grass. As we walked, we sank in almost up to our knees.

Ina and my father hardly said a word about his parents. In fact, they hardly spoke at all. I guess they were simply too overwhelmed by the miracle of each other's physical presence.

Ina told the story about how the doctor who delivered her had come by horse and buggy and had to return by sleigh.

She noted the names of the flowers we found. Queen Anne's lace. Reindeer moss. Pursewarren.

My father found an old piece of quartz.

Most was said by silence. There was no mention of my father's mother.

That night, when we got back to our motel, my father was ashen with exhaustion. Because it was still early, I suggested that I go into town so he could sleep. Instead, he began to talk. He went on for hours. I knew he was simply trying to keep me there with him.

He told me about how he and his brother used to massage his foster mother's feet. I asked him about her prudishness. He explained that someone had once told him that she was physically too small to give satisfaction to her husband and that this had given her a feeling of guilt that she had never been able to get over.

Then he told me a story about how he had once persuaded the chauffeur's daughter to undress for him. The chauffeur, named Norris, had caught them together and made my father tell his foster mother. His conversation with "Muddie" went like this:

Muddie: "Oh. Oh. Oh. My God. Oh. Oh. Did you touch her?"

Matthew: "Maybe."

Muddie: "Oh. Oh. Oh. You've got to give Norris all your war bonds to make up for it."

I could hardly believe my ears. Didn't he remember? Almost the same thing had happened between us when I was thirteen. Why hadn't he been more understanding then? When I asked my father about it, he claimed he couldn't remember that incident. Yet the boy whom I had bribed to take nude photos of his sister is now the doctor who treats him in his old age.

He still thinks about his brother and his foster mother every night before he goes to bed.

For the first time he really told me about his career. But it was more than that. His career was his real life. The life I never knew about. His foster mother told him that, if he didn't want to work with his brains, he should work with his hands. So she sent him to Wentworth Institute, where my father discovered his true love. "A place to find out how things worked." He would even go in on Saturday to use the machines.

He never went to college, but he came to be accepted as a very accomplished electrical and mechanical engineer. He learned by asking questions. By always biting off more than he could chew.

In every job he had, there was always an older man who took an interest in him. Though I don't say anything, it occurs to me that my father in one way or another always found some man who would be willing to act as his father.

It is a revelation to hear him talk about his career. He is in complete charge of it. He is no patsy as I had always believed. He is crafty and determined. Somehow he always manages to get what he wants. It is an entirely different side to him. I had only seen him with my mother, where he was more of a child than a man.

Later we talked about women. On his first job he had to go all around New England, repairing nurses' call systems. He would never "have anything to do with the kind of women who went after men."

He told me a story about a woman who tried to seduce him. He put her off and the husband found out. For a while, my father thought the husband would appreciate it. Later, the man stole an invention of my father's and patented it under his own name. For years afterward, the man used to come over to the house about once a month, drunk and weeping with remorse.

I asked my father if there had been other women. He replied with great scorn, "Several of them tried."

His one true love was my mother. He credits her with everything that he has become. "I wouldn't have been anything without Mother."

But she never told him about the existence of Virginia, her older sister.

I asked him about what he thought had happened between us when I was growing up. He explained that my mother had taken over completely, and there was nothing he could do about it.

Later, he explained further that he had given up on me completely when I had been caught, at the tail end of World War II, selling black market cigarettes in high school.

"I didn't have any time for those shenanigans."

We went on talking until late in the night.

When I finally got into bed, I couldn't get his words out of my head. *I gave up on you. I didn't have any time for those shenanigans.*

But in the morning those words no longer seemed to make any difference. As we were parting from each other at the station, my father turned to me and said, "You should marry a good little girl like Martha."

And so, in spite of everything else, my father has always continued to regard my mother as that beautiful young girl he once saved from a terrible fate. And, in spite of everything, in spite of a lifetime of camouflage, the reality is that my mother allowed herself to be saved. Because in the end my father has always come through. Always supported her and provided for the children. He never failed her.

At the deepest level he always came through with what she needed. This is the bedrock of their relationship. The reason why they have survived. I think my father knows it. Probably they both know. Even though they have never admitted it to themselves.

Their gratitude to each other. Their gratefulness hidden under so many layers of denial and self-denial. My father's gratitude to my mother for being allowed to take care of her. For bearing his children. For staying with him.

My mother's gratitude for being saved. For being cared about. For being taken care of. It is so hard for her to admit that gratitude. But my father knows. It is hard for me also to see her gratitude. How could it be otherwise? She won't acknowledge it even to herself. She does everything to hide it from herself and from him. No one seems more ungracious, more unfeeling. I have certainly been fooled into believing in the depth of her scorn of him. But in the end, he knows. In spite of a lifetime of indications to the contrary. In spite of all her efforts to convince herself. In the core of himself, he knows.

What a thing. The real lives of people and their apparent lives. It is hard for a child to understand. So easy to be fooled by the surface of things. So easy to be fooled by the surface of our own lives. So hard to live the deepest parts of ourselves in our daily life. To have our love undisguised from ourselves and from each other.

No wonder my mother finds it hard to admit her love for my father. How could she help but feel that if she did, it would simply be taken away from her? He would be taken away from her and killed just like her father and her mother and her sister.

The only way she can protect her love for herself, protect my father from the lethal effects of her love, is to hide her love from everyone. Perhaps most of all, from herself.

What an incredible revelation. My mother dearly loves my father. She always has. She probably has never stopped loving him from the very beginning. And I never really knew. Or at least I could never admit it to myself until now. I knew about his love but not about hers. What a change in my own perception of life. Because I don't think I have ever believed in the love of a woman for a man before. Never believed that I could ever be loved by a woman. What a way to begin tomorrow. To believe in love. To believe in the love of men and women for each other.

⇁

It has been almost two years since our trip to Maine together. My father doesn't go to work anymore. My mother never goes out of the house anymore. Some days the pain of her arthritis is so bad that she just sits in her chair all day, crying.

My father does all the shopping now. He is very proud of his marketing ability. When I go out to visit them, he displays his cans and bottles and waxed-cardboard cartons as if they were precious works of art.

He also does all the cooking now. He wasn't an engineer all his life for nothing. No waste motion. Every step is carefully thought out and planned far in advance. My mother talks about his feats in the kitchen as if he were an infant prodigy.

"He goes to the market every week. He's so cute. He knows just where to get everything. He has the whole week planned out."

And there is just the faintest hint of ridicule in her voice. But he doesn't mind. He understands how hard it has become for her, and how difficult it has always been for her to accept anything graciously.

After he has finished cooking, he brings her food to her on a tray. Spry chipper old nursy. When they have finished supper, he does all the dishes in a special way he has. And he seems to be grateful just to be allowed to wait on her. At last he has found a way to be wanted. To give. This is the first time he has ever had an unmixed sense of his importance to her. Before, she always made him feel as if he were a threatening stranger who had tricked her into marriage.

Now all that has changed. My father has finally come out of the cellar. It is his house and his kitchen now. She is the boarder. At the very end of his life, he has finally emerged from darkness and isolation. Perhaps that is why he seems so frolicsome. He has been freed after a lifetime of captivity in a prison where the only other inmates were machines: lathes, drill presses, milling machines, grinders, razor-sharp cutting tools and their glittering spore, heaps of bronze and iron and steel curls that littered the floor. Now he has found a way out, into all the domesticity he never had before, the warmth of the oven and the mystery of soap bubbles.

Sometimes he calls his wife "Martha." But most of the time he calls her "Mother." Sometimes he calls her by his foster mother's nicknames, "Little Mother" and "Muddie." My mother just calls him "Matt."

She never stops reminding him that they don't have any money. And that he was a failure because he never did earn money. She always does this in front of me. And she has even said things like this in front of my children. But my father acknowledges no malice in what she says.

"But, Mother," he will reply with sweet gentleness, "you don't understand. It's not how much money you make. It's the satisfaction that you get from your work that matters."

But my mother always manages to have the last word.

"Well, Matt, it would be nice to have a little money now and then to buy some of the things we need."

There is nothing more to say after that.

He is very kind and never reminds her that she has willfully spent every penny he has made, just as soon as she could get her hands on it. That money was like a curse to her and she couldn't get rid of it fast enough. And that, if there was ever any of it left over, it preyed on her mind until she could find a way to get rid of it.

He doesn't need to remind her because he is happier than he ever has been in his whole life. And in some strange way she is happier too, even though she spends whole days crying.

More than anything else, it is the disappearance of sex that has freed them. My mother doesn't have to feel threatened by her imagination of my father's sensuality. My father isn't ravaged by frustration. They never touch. It is as if there were a *cordon sani-*

taire between them. He never tries to kiss her, never holds her hand, or even puts his arm around her. He never even brushes up against her in passing. All his love goes into his precise ceremonies of nursely care. He has learned the limits of their relationship and he wants no more cutting reminders of the depth of my mother's fear of him and his masculine sensuality. He knows her aversion is still there. He knows not to test it anymore, because he has accepted that it will always be there.

So, without anything else to do, their concerns are limited to matters having to do with the house. Regulating the temperature. Getting up and down stairs. Preparing their meals. And, because they are old, even the simplest of arrangements requires a great deal of care and preparation and thought. Everything they want from the upstairs has to be taken down in the morning, because they can't manage to go up the stairs more than once a day. And, because my father can't physically manage to get to the store more than once a week, his one trip has to suffice.

That trip has already taken on the mythological significance of an odyssey. I think that my father feels like a great hunter going out on a weekly trek for food. They both talk about it as if he were going on a long and perilous journey. Will the car hold up? Will my father have an accident? Other people drive so recklessly. Will he have enough money?

And they also talk endlessly about my father's increasing mastery of the mysteries of shopping. He is becoming a very canny shopper. They also talk about his stubbornness. If my mother asks him to get something he doesn't like, he simply forgets it. Years before, this might have been the trigger for a deadly fight. Now it is just a charming foible of the great hunter.

Most times, he takes another old couple shopping with him. He pretends to do it against his will. He complains about them. They never offer him any money for gas (of course, he wouldn't take it if they did). They exploit him by taking him out of his way to stores where he doesn't want to go. Once the old man had the gall to ask my father to wait for him while he got a haircut. My father pretends to be outraged. My mother and father talk bitterly about the injustice of it. But secretly, I think, they are both delighted. The suggestion of exploitation adds a dash of adventure and spice to a trip which is, after all, their only direct experience of the outside world.

Somehow that trip has to last a whole week, not just in terms of what my father is able to buy. That trip is life itself and the events and anecdotes and bits of overheard conversation have to be made to last. How my father was treated by the salespeople. What the sights were on the way back and forth. New horror stories about high prices. The wondrous foods they could eat if only they could afford them.

Once I went with him on one of his outings. He is so humble and polite. So curious and gracious. Eyes twinkling because he is excited to be out. Wanting it to be the grand social occasion it needs to be. Trying to slow it down so it won't go too fast. Asking everyone how they are and hoping for really long, detailed replies. In return, being very slow and precise about himself. His heart lifting with joy when someone thinks to ask him about his wife. Because he does have a wife. He is not just living for himself alone. Whenever he can, he throws out shy little conversational gambits. "I see that . . ." But he is old and therefore of little consequence in our world. Everyone has so much to do. Who has the time to stop to talk to an old man? But my father understands. He doesn't ask for much.

As he has grown older, it is as if a veil has been lifted from his life. Now he can see and feel all those things he was too busy or too afraid to let himself experience before. Now he really sees the textures and colors of all the vegetables and fruits. The glossy purple of eggplants. The bronze of pineapples. And I see him really looking into people's faces. Everything seems wondrous to him, the way it must have been when he was a child and just beginning to see. All those intervening years of darkness have passed away. Particularly the business of working. Now there is nothing to prevent him from seeing and his eyes have finally opened. And the supermarket, even under the fluorescent lights, is as wonderful and strange as a medieval bazaar. My father is at the helm of his shopping cart. And all the other carts maneuver around him with their own steersmen at their helms.

He smiles at all the young girls. They don't threaten him any-more with their suggestions of sexuality because he can see right through them to the heart of their enormous innocence. The sight of it, its proximity, makes him almost want to swoon. All around him, little gaggles of girls, conspiring, giggling, displaying them-selves to anyone who wants to see. See me! See me! See me the way I want to be seen and not any other way.

The girls look away shyly when my father smiles at them. The boys frighten him because they are so impetuous. Any instant they might rear up like tidal waves, and sweep him and his cart into oblivion. So he hugs the wall very closely whenever he hears them or sees them nearby.

And having so many people all around him makes him almost giddy after a week of isolation. He finds himself breaking out in smiles. And he cautions himself to be more careful. He has to remember to restrain his joy because it is all out of proportion to what anyone else would understand.

When he is in the vicinity of other old people, he drops anchor and passes the time of day. "Are you getting enough heat?" "I hope we don't get any more snow." "My knee is really acting up." But the exact words aren't important. They already know every-thing there is to know about each other. They are old. What more is there to know? So sometimes they just stand there, silently glowing for each other.

My father is a very precise shopper. He examines every pur-chase. It has to be just right. No blemishes to mar its perfection. As he stands there, I can see him relishing the touch of things and savoring the mysterious thrill of potential ownership.

And he is very much aware of his special responsibility. He has to think not only of himself but also of his wife. There always has to be a surprise for her. Something unexpected and wonderful to thrill and delight her. He watches the growing collection of won-ders in his cart like a mother hen surveying her brood of chicks. He buys more and more treats these days, because it is really more necessary now to be happy than to live a long life. There have never been enough parties. Just imagine Mr. Matthew Armstrong in the old days buying potato chips and cupcakes. Sometimes he must even be grinning at himself at the sheer improbability of such an occurrence.

Sometimes he can't find something he has written down on his list. He experiences a sudden shock of terror. Don't they have it anymore? Could they have moved it to another aisle? Finally getting up the nerve to ask a clerk. Scared that the clerk might not notice him. Realizing that his voice is very soft now. Feeling himself to be very thin and almost translucent. Any snub is like a harbinger of death because his sense of his own life is so tenuous. Thinking sometimes: *Am I alive or am I dead?* Finally locating a sympathetic clerk. Trying to keep the desperate need out of his voice (remembering that this trip has to last a whole week, and his wife is depending on him). Realizing that no one else, particularly no one so young as the clerk, could ever understand his sense of urgency. The last thing he wants is to be made fun of.

The clerk replies: "Sorry, we're out of that. Try again tomorrow." But my father's tomorrow is a week away, and who knows if he will last that long? Or the clerk might say: "I don't know. You had better ask someone else." Or a miracle might happen. Could it be anything less than a miracle? The clerk volunteers to get the needed item from the back.

"You don't have to bother."

"Oh, no bother at all. It will just take a minute."

"That's really very nice of you. I don't get a chance to get out very often, and my wife really wanted those."

But sometimes there is no miracle. The item he really needs isn't there. And there is no one to get it for him. He has to struggle to ward off his disappointment. He doesn't want it to spoil his whole trip. His heart starts to flutter. He knows he has to regain his composure. There are still many choices and decisions to make. So much depends on him. Anyone standing close to him at these moments of extreme stress could hear him panting. They could also hear a strange little metallic whistle, like a tiny teapot boiling. If they were curious, they might look around for the little child with his toy whistle. But it would only be my father trying to catch his breath.

Sometimes one of the other old people will get mad and start arguing with a clerk or another customer. And their harsh voices cut at my father's ears. He looks away and tries not to pay any attention to them and tries to wash the ugliness from his mind. Because that isn't the right way to behave and he doesn't want to get infected by it. Disturbances like that can be contagious. Sometimes, in one of those endless aisles, he might encounter a weird crazy man, clothing all askew, fly open, rat's-nest wig alop on his head. Eyeballs tearing out of their sockets. And after the first shock of fear, my father feels like crying. Because all old men have become his brothers. His special race of people. He adjusts himself like a retriever shaking off water, and stands up straighter than before. Sticking his chin up in the air and wheeling his cart on by, still shivering from the chill of madness.

Going on until his purchases are almost completed and everything on the list is bought. Now all that remains is the special treat which will make the light in Mother's eyes shine.

"Oh, Matt. You're wonderful. How did you ever think of that?" He's waited all his life to hear those words. Waited almost fifty years. Waited through the birth of two sons. Through six different jobs. Through countless thousands of hours of grinding labor. Sometimes eighteen hours a day. Waited in bed when they still slept together, during those times when she would let him make love to her with her body rigid and unyielding. Waited. Waited. Waited. But those words never came. She would never give them to him. But now all that has changed. And it is wonderful.

And the expectation of those words is like a billowing cloud gently wafting him along those corridors of towering boxes. It is so wonderful to hear those words now that it doesn't matter that he has had to wait fifty years for them.

He knows what makes her happy now. He knows about her sweet tooth. What will it be this time? Last week it had been six different flavors of cupcakes. The week before that, it had been a special new coffee cake. This week the pies look good. But what would be the best? He knows how much she likes apple, but they have had it so often that it wouldn't be a treat. Now cherry, that would be more like it. So tart and red and festive. It feels so right when he picks it up in his hands that his face breaks into a big smile. He puts it right on top in the middle like a crown on all his other purchases. Later, at the check-out counter, he will be very careful to separate it from everything else, so it won't be crushed.

I've also been with my mother while she waits for him to return. She still pretends not to care. But she sits in that empty house, listening for the sound of his car. And it is as if her ears were carved out and empty, just waiting to be filled with that sound and none other.

Her whole being concentrates on the expectation of it. Everything, all her other senses, are temporarily suspended. She tries to distract herself. A book. A newspaper. Thinking about her sons. But her mind won't give her any peace. All her attempts to diminish her ears' aching need only serves to make her more aware of it. When her mind wanders even for an instant, it is suddenly snapped back. Because the stillness of the house reminds her of his death.

She has told me that she believes he will die first, and leave her alone. She has already begun to hold it against him a little bit. She tries to believe that she will have to endure his absence for only an hour or two. But some part of herself is convinced that he will be gone for an eternity. And she tells herself that she needs him only to take care of her. He is not important except for the buying of the food and the preparation of the meals. She is still unwilling to admit, after all these years, that she, a woman, needs him, a man. Oh, he had a duty to perform all those years. He had to work and make money so she could be a mother and make her nest and nurture her children. But it was his duty and she had no qualms whatsoever about exacting it from him.

She still can't admit that they have grown so close together over the years that now they are almost the same person. That, without knowing it, she hasn't been herself in that separate, discreet, superior way she has always prided herself on for years and years. That, for decades perhaps, almost since the very beginning, she hasn't been just Martha. That each year her sense of herself has become more and more congruent with her husband's being, until now she has no self except what she shares with him, the self they share together.

And so she really waits there for the safe return of a part of herself that has temporarily departed from her. And she fights against the full realization of her dependency on him. Because all their life together, she has been the loved one. She has taken the gift of his adoration as her due and she has scorned to return it or reward it in any way. But now, grudgingly, she finds herself admiring him. After all, he still goes out into the world. And he has acquired a deep source of strength that she never was aware of before. She doesn't know where he has gotten it from. And she begrudges him that too. Because, somehow, he acquired it without her knowledge. And he is really too satisfied with himself and what he has done in the world.

He was good to her and she appreciated that, but still it was only her due, in return for all her sufferings and deprivations over the years. She was the important one. Why didn't people seem to realize it now, the way they used to? After all, she had just been a young girl when they had married. Who knows what she could have been if she had had her chance? She could have married other men. Some of them were actually rich now. And her husband had tricked her into marrying him. She thought he had been rich. He had certainly seemed to be. But it turned out he was the poorest and the neediest person in the world. How could she help not feeling deprived and frustrated, after all these years of people telling her how beautiful she was and how she could have been an actress or something like that if she had wanted to be?

But, sitting there, straining to hear the sound of his return, the crunching of the gravel in the driveway as he turns in from the street, as if he were turning his ship into a cove and beaching it in the teeming surf, she can almost admit to herself that she has failed to get something from him. That he could have given her much more if she had only given him the chance. At this thought, she winces as if a sudden chill wind had blown through the house. Why hadn't he made her do it? Why hadn't he forced her to accept him? Why hadn't he broken her? Beaten her? Because that was what she had needed. Why had he always sat back and waited all these years for her to ask for it? Didn't he know that she could never bring herself to ask for it? That he had to force her because her need for it was too great? That, if he did ask for it, she would only have to deny him? He had to take it from her. She was a wild horse that had to be broken.

Of course, not a word of this appears in her consciousness. The only sign of its presence is that cold chill. For a few minutes, she imagines that she might be getting sick, catching the flu or something. She flutters and huddles into herself to discover some elusive body-healing warmth. *I wish he would get back soon. I hope nothing happens to him. He is so old and sometimes I know he doesn't drive as carefully as he should.*

And in her mind she already sees him almost as a ghost. A mere wisp of light at the helm of an enormous thundering machine, veering up into the sky like Icarus's chariot.

The wind outside dislodges an ash can cover and sends it careering down the street. And in her mind she sees a terrible explosion. Dozens of cars crashing into each other, explosions flaring up into the night sky. Men in flames running in the darkness like phosphorus flares. The image comes and goes. It wasn't his car she heard rounding the corner. Something about the sound wasn't right. And she scolds herself for forgetting to think about him in the right way. For letting her mind stray and become impure. Because it seems to her as if it were her expectation of him and not his car or the gasoline that is actually bringing him home. If she lets her mind stray, he might get into trouble. And thinking about how she is actually bringing him home, she smiles in expectation of his return, hoping that everything has gone all right. That he found everything he wanted to buy and that he had enough money and that everyone had treated him with respect. And that he didn't get into any fights, because she still remembers his awful temper. Trying to reassure herself that, if anything happened, someone would be sure to call her. Wishing that she could get up from her chair so that she could stand at the window and watch for him. But she can stand for only a few seconds at a time. And she couldn't keep getting up and down. Why is he taking so long? He really is such a sweet old man. He is really very precious. Sometimes she has to fight so hard not to really love him.

As she thinks of him in the market doing all his little things, he seems so wonderful. But she can't let herself say that she loves him. It is absolutely forbidden to her. She doesn't know why. It just is. She can never let herself think, even to herself, that she loves him. Those words can never be allowed to enter her head, or something awful would happen. Of course, she could never say those words to him.

Sometimes she was just able to check herself in time. She would sense the feeling rising up in her like a jet of warm water. And it would be all she could do to turn it off before it was too late. What would happen if she did actually forget herself and say those forbidden words? No, it was too awful even to think of. It was unthinkable. With those words, she would be denying everything she was. Everything she had been. It would be completely shameless. Like letting his rough coarse hands actually penetrate her body, letting them grope around inside her very heart. She didn't belong to him. She didn't belong to any man. She never would.

And what if she could actually see herself as she is at this very instant in time, and realize how faintly she exists in this darkened room? Realize that she is just a mere wisp of being, huddled on the corner of a torn couch. No more than a faintly fluttering heart. Would that change the way she feels? Probably not.

Everything still seems so important to her, particularly that moral struggle that goes on inside her every day of her life. That battle of pride fought in every joint of her body. It is all so important. Yet, in fact, she barely exists. She is just a flickering light. Would it make any difference to her if she knew? Would she be able to give up at last and finally love? Pull back a little ways, and she would be barely detectable in that room. Forget to look at her, even for an instant, and she would probably disappear altogether. If only she could disappear to herself. Then, perhaps, she could let herself love.

It is getting very close to the time now. It is particularly important now to pretend that she doesn't care. It is excruciatingly hard. But it is essential if everything is to be all right. You never get anything you want in this life unless you are able to convince the forces of fate that you really don't care. That you don't want what you need so desperately.

But before she even has the chance to make her offering of indifference, he is there. The sound of his return is over almost even before it begins. She feels almost as if she has been cheated, because it hasn't lasted longer and she hasn't been able to worry about it quite as much as she would like. Even sitting inside the house, she can feel the force and pull, the whirlpool, of his return. And she has to get closer to it. She adjusts the position of her cane on the arm of the couch and begins to rock back and forth, trying to work up enough momentum for that final spring to her feet. One. Two. Three. It works! She is on her feet. Oh, God, did that hurt.

Moving as fast as she can, she rushes to the door that leads in from the garage, where he is sure to appear. Needing desperately to be there. Adjusting the look on her face to express her physical pain and the ordeal of being there to greet him. Lowering her face and looking up as if she were a child about to start bawling. And it really does hurt terribly. That is no lie. But she has to display her pain in the right way.

She gets there just in time to hear the outer door open and his footsteps cross the small outer hall. The door in front of her opens. And such a force, like a tornado, seems to enter the room. There he stands, overcoat swimming all around his age-shrunken body, eyes too tired even to focus, ashen-faced, wheezing from the strain of carrying in the packages. His whole face twinkling when he sees her standing there waiting for him.

"You didn't have to meet me, Mother." Wagging himself with pleasure like an old dog. Shivering with pleasure like an old dog.

"Did everything go all right, Matt? Did you find everything you wanted?" Making her voice pathetic and prematurely ready for utter disappointment. Telling him with the curious sign language of her body that she knows nothing ever goes right and that she is ready to understand the very worst. But he can't even see her or really hear her, because he is so buoyant with victory.

"Just let me put these down, Mother." Moving around her to the counter. "You should see what I got." Taking his purchases from the bag with a magician's flourish. Displaying them to her one by one, still trying to catch his breath but so excited that he can't wait.

Already starting to tell her about everything that has happened to him since he last saw her. Holding back just enough so that his stories will last. Both of them so excited by the look of their new possessions actually in their house. By the sounds of the cans on the linoleum counter and the crinkling of the cellophane bags.

"But did you get any . . ."

"Oh, yes, I did. Look right over here." Getting down to the bottom of one bag and going out to the car for the other one. Bringing out the surprise very nonchalantly. His wife seeing it. Her face lighting up.

"Oh, Matt! A cherry pie. We haven't had one of those for ages. You're so wonderful."

He takes a deep breath and smiles, his whole body shuddering with exhaustion. He shakes his head at the wonder of it all. In the silence, they can both hear the sound of his whistling.

My father now at last has a mother completely to himself. My mother now has a father. In a very real sense, they have both become their very own parents. The parents they never had.